FRAGILE MAGIC

A Guidebook for Theatre Respondents

by
Ronald A. Willis

Focus Publishing
R. Pullins Co.
Newburyport, MA

TABLE OF CONTENTS

How the approach to theatre response developed and why this book.

Fragile magic and the difficulty it poses for meaningful communication.
Theatre respondents face challenges. Production companies profess different
goals. Performance styles differ. Performance-centric focus. Imagination
is key. Live theatre's uniqueness. Points of Fragility in the formulation and
perception of a performance. Artistic Synergism. The magic smothered. A
caution.

Complex and diverse audiences. The respondent defined. Respondents as fellow
theatre artists. Assumptions about theatre events. The empirical performance.
The performance image. Preparing to witness the performance.

Components of the theatre event. Para-aesthetics. Para-aesthetic effects. The
respondent and para-aesthetics.

Collaboration for perception. The collaborators. The spectator's challenge.
Theatre's many faces. The variable nature of theatrical performance.
Performance text. The ever-changing "now". Performance text and written
script. Penetrating the guiding thought. Other than script bases for
performance. Spectator obligations.

Getting under way. Your feedback. Others' feedback. Description of what
you perceived. The three foci of non-valuative description: The fictive world.
Theatrical means. Your reactions to the fictive world. Empowering developing
theatre artists to be self-actuating.

The evaluation challenge. Tapping into and stimulating the creative process.
Evaluate para-aesthetic concerns as factors. Theatrical performance offers
experience. Remaining open-minded. The theatre respondent's special
niche. Advice couched as suggestions rather than edicts. Immediacy. Self
determination. Clarity. Harmony. Boldness. Virtuosity. What's in it for you.

Offers responses to some frequently posed questions aspiring respondents
have.

Theatre Respondent Guide review notes.

ACKNOWLEDGEMENTS

Given the fact that it has taken me so long to set down my thoughts about theatre response on pages others could access, it would be foolhardy for me to try to list all those people who have influenced and helped me come to the conclusions I now hold. Certainly my fellow respondents for the Kennedy Center American College Theatre Festival are among them, as are all the people who labored in my workshops. And there are many others, including my teaching colleagues at the University of Kansas and my family. But no one deserves acknowledgement and thanks more than my wife Marie. She has both heard and read every word of every draft of this work—repeatedly. I am undyingly grateful for, among other things, her patience, her insights and her detailed advice. I'm churlishly tempted to say that if you find any shortcomings here you should blame them on her. But that would be an ungrateful lie of the highest magnitude.

PREFACE

HOW THE APPROACH TO THEATRE RESPONSE DEVELOPED AND
WHY THIS BOOK

This book is personal for me. For nearly four decades I have offered
uncounted formal responses to high school, college, and community theatre
performances. The responses were intended to help the people who assembled and executed the performances find ways to improve their efforts.
I had varying degrees of success. I watched other respondents undertake
similar assignments and compile more or less similar records.

I was moved to think about what it was we were (or should be) attempting to accomplish as respondents and what might be considered a successful response. I came to accept the idea that our principle task was to help
developing theatre artists understand what they had already accomplished
and to provide them with the wherewithal to improve their future work.
That's it in a nutshell.

I set about crafting an approach which would do this in a reasonably
consistent fashion. I discovered that what I gradually came up with not
only helped me, but other respondents and aspiring respondents as well.
Some of my early musings on the subject even showed up, sometimes to
my complete surprise, in newsletters and internet communiqués. People
of varying backgrounds openly testified to their usefulness.

Eventually I offered response workshops in regional meetings, national
conventions and theatre festivals all around the country. I found the approach I espoused, which I continued to refine, helped highly perceptive
respondents voice insights in ways that lots of people found effective. The
same basic approach also enabled novices and people with limited theatre
backgrounds to provide something of value and to avoid some pitfalls that
might be counterproductive. Moreover, both these groups of people were
able to grow and learn from their response efforts.

I also discovered something else. Much of the foundational work that
informed the ways respondents went about their tasks proved to be very

useful for serious-minded audience members. Spectators who wanted theatre performances to be illuminating and transformative, who wanted to get the most vivid experiences and most telling understanding from their attendance at live theatre events, could discipline their viewing and thinking habits in highly beneficial ways. In essence they found they could hone their audience spectatorship abilities and avoid some of the pitfalls that often plague theatre-goers by following the training steps undertaken by theatre respondents.

Over the years many people (teachers, students, general audience members and respondents) have asked for this response system to be described and its principles to be set forth in a book. I don't know why I delayed, but finally I am honoring their requests. Most of all, I intend this to be a guidebook which stimulates discussion about the theory and practice of theatre response (and perhaps theatre in general) and helps respondents serve the needs and interests of developing theatre artists at any level of accomplishment. But clearly I intend to help developing audience members share in the profit wherever they can.

Of course my personal perspectives on theatre, the nature of perception (especially of theatre), the place of the respondent in the overall theatrical process and how these things influence one another are woven all though what I say. I don't expect everyone to agree with all the details of my views or to accept whole-heartedly my formulations and preferences. But those perspectives have pretty much worked for me, and I am told that they often work for others. I can only hope that people who read this guidebook will find them at least mildly interesting and perhaps even useful and satisfying. I believe they can prepare you to be an effective respondent. I guess we'll finally see.

1

ENCOUNTERING THE FRAGILE MAGIC

FRAGILE MAGIC AND THE DIFFICULTY IT POSES FOR MEANINGFUL COMMUNICATION

Live theatrical performance—at its best—is magical. It displays the kind of magic that informs every truly mesmerizing theatre experience. On those happy occasions when it is especially evident the artists, craftspeople and technicians who create the performance, along with the fortunate audiences who witness and partake of its power, are fond of saying "the performance works."

What they mean, of course, is that the performance satisfies them at a profound personal level. It proceeds as if animated by its own internal force. It creates an experience they embrace, even though it is often one they cannot fully explain in words. They nonetheless report sensing that the performance has a life of its own. Events flow naturally and organically. Nothing seems contrived or manipulative. Any intellectual partitions that might, under other circumstances, separate elements within the performance seem to disappear, or at least become insignificant. Time passes quickly and effortlessly. The whole is held together by the power of a vicarious experience, an experience the spectators attribute to their performance viewing. If questioned they are likely to assess the performance as well conceived, carefully crafted, and precisely executed. But at heart they are really responding to the fullness and richness of their own inner experience. The comments they make that target aspects of the performance are really afterthoughts of a sort, justifications (and usually marginally satisfying explanations) for how they feel. Nonetheless, when reflecting on their experiences later, everyone who was deeply moved by a performance testifies to the fact that at that particular performance something special happened, the performance really worked. It was magical.

The magic associated with live theatrical performance is undeniably powerful and can be transformative, but it is surprisingly fragile. It is also mercurial. It frequently has far from uniform impact among different members of the same audience or even among the ranks of those who shaped the performance. It may be totally absent for some, while others testify to its strong presence. Multiple performances within the run of a single production can easily vary markedly from one another when their relative "magic" is appraised. It is deflating to realize that many performances simply do not work—at least not as fully as the practitioners and spectators who are involved with them might wish they would. It may still be that brief glimpses during a performance suggest the promise of magic. But if that promise only operates intermittently or is insufficiently strong, the performance is likely to be adjudged, at best, as merely satisfactory or promising—in short, more or less disappointing.

Many of us who are active in theatre want to do what we can to increase the power and frequency of theatre's fragile magic. One effective way to do that is to focus our attention on the work of the theatre practitioners, especially those who regard themselves (and whom others regard) as **developing theatre artists**. We can provide them with the kind of detailed and focused feedback they can use in crafting subsequent performances. All across the country theatre people, especially in educational and community theatres, do this when they serve as **performance respondents**. Their goal as respondents is to help theatre practitioners improve and exercise meaningful control of their live theatre practice. To that end they attend local productions as well as those performed at regional and national theatre festivals to provide meaningful analyses and appraisals of performance practice. I presume you may want to join their ranks—that is, if you have not already done so. This guidebook can help you.

THEATRE RESPONDENTS FACE CHALLENGES

Make no mistake. The task of serving as an effective theatre respondent is a formidable one. Theatre performance cannot be approached from a "one size fits all" perspective. Theatre as a whole is a diversified enterprise characterized by different goals, practices, and levels of accomplishment. For example, the goals of different **performance teams** (such teams consisting of the many people who actively shape a particular performance) are far from uniform. Moreover, they serve a range of divergent audiences that have varying preferences and tastes. Consequently the dynamics of the performances created to serve each of these audiences exhibit bold differences. A respondent's approach in offering feedback, if it is to truly serve the needs of diverse performance teams, must take that variety into account and find ways to resonate to it. Similarly, a general audience member is likely to be a spectator at many different kinds of performance and is also challenged to adjust to the diverse traits they exhibit.

PRODUCTION COMPANIES PROFESS DIFFERENT GOALS

Even a brief sampling of the kinds of theatre enterprises you probably are familiar with shows plenty of diversity when it comes to the ways they define their goals.

1. Some performance teams focus their principal energies on creating theatre events that have the power to imaginatively transport spectators, at least those who are willing and able, to exciting times and places, often to another era or culture. In such an undertaking the teams often set out to acquaint audiences with characters and events literally not of this world. For their part audience members may vicariously indulge in exciting and sometimes even dangerous experiences, the kind typically denied them in their real world lives.

2. Other performance teams pursue goals with a carefully defined educational focus, such as one which illuminates aspects of the human condition in compelling ways so as to awaken attendees to previously undreamt-of possibilities. They challenge their audiences to consider life options that were previously unthinkable.

3. Of course many who engage in live performance set out to entertain audiences by diverting them with no far-reaching intention of expanding their intellectual or spiritual horizons. Often they do this through the display of virtuosity, cleverness, or sheer high energy. They strive to make the spectators forget their personal anxieties and problems, if only for a brief time. Typically they try to invoke the kind of laughter that provides an emotional respite fueled by the belief that people can then return to their "real lives" refreshed and revitalized.

4. Often performances overtly endorse the existing values and feelings of an audience and do not try to challenge them to embrace new perceptions. Instead they revisit, often in a sentimental fashion, beliefs the viewers already possess. Undoubtedly many audiences experience a feeling of comfort

when they immerse their imaginations in familiar emotional and intellectual surroundings. They feel their existing world views are strengthened.

It perhaps goes without saying that neither audiences nor performances are as neatly and discretely stratified as the above brief descriptions might seem to indicate. Individual performance goals and audience responses are almost always a complex mix of what is possible. As a result, any given performance can provide its audience with a rich overlay of theatrically derived experiences.

PERFORMANCE STYLES DIFFER

Not only do the goals of particular performance teams differ from one another, the styles and performance techniques they employ do as well. Sometimes the choice of script might be seen as the key determinant of any team's performance style, but such is not always the case. If you reflect on your own theatre experiences you will undoubtedly agree that any script is susceptible to being approached by a particular performance team from a unique interpretive perspective. The result can be a style and an array of practices that are performance-specific rather than script-specific. Respondents face the challenge of adjusting to whatever style and theatrical practices the performance exemplifies.

PERFORMANCE-CENTRIC FOCUS

It is also worth noting early in our discussion that the words of a theatre text simply do not carry the full weight of a performance's meaning or power. If they did, it would follow that any recitation of a script's words would be equivalent to any other recitation. Every "performance" of a particular script would be equivalent. But that is clearly not the case. Taking our cue from that fact, our principal, but not exclusive, focus is on **performance-centric** matters. It is here that most of the fragile magic of theatre is made manifest.

Respondents and spectators are called upon to be flexible. Certainly performances that are geared to be realistic, or approximately so, call for a responsive sensibility that is different from that which would be appropriate for a highly abstract expressionistic performance which sets aside the normal parameters of quotidian life. The presence of music, singing and dancing in a performance sets it apart from one that is exclusively verbal. The appropriation of evident and specialized theatrical conventions expands the range of performance styles. Certainly asides, direct address and even direct contact with an audience are traditional techniques that are easily recognized and accepted by many theatre-goers. Less frequently encountered are such things as a single character being portrayed by more than one actor (sometimes simultaneously), the integration of electronically mediated and real time stimuli, the expressive use of racial and gender traits that become relevant to characterization in a wide variety of ways, and a host of other theatrical strategies that expand the palette of expression. The respondent's challenge is to forge an effective way of approaching performances that will allow each performance's style and practice to exercise its own, perhaps unanticipated, manner of accessing the theatre experience.

IMAGINATION IS KEY

But no matter what goal is pursued, what audience benefit is derived, what styles and techniques are pursued, live theatre performance, especially at its magical best, always thrives on the exercise of imagination. Moreover, it does so at every juncture from its inception to its execution. It is imagination that provides the motive force to marshal the sensitive insights and diverse talents of the skilled theatre artists and craftspeople who form the performance team. We can readily identify the writers, composers, directors, choreographers, designers, and actors. Often there are other specialists as well. It is the disciplined exercise of their imaginations that enables them to meld their efforts into the focused artifact that a live performance eventually becomes.

It is also imagination that excites and extends the enlivened responses of capable and willing theatre audiences. During the actual time and space-bound theatre event, the imagination of audience members, fueled by the actual performance, completes the arc that allows the theatre experience to be magical—that makes the theatrical performance "work." Effective theatre respondents and spectators have to exercise a healthy regard for the workings of imagination.

Certainly no one can claim that live theatrical performance has exclusive dominion over people's imagination. The free and expansive exercise of imagination characterizes the best work displayed in every human endeavor and it makes potent the responsive understanding of any auditor. It is especially evident, for example, that other art and entertainment forms closely related to live theatre performance share many of the same strategies and practices. Films, videos, books and even video games are viewed by many people as virtual analogs to live theatre—at least insofar as the private experience of them is concerned. Certainly these theatre-like forms also share a considerable number of similar imagination-driven strategies and they employ a host of similar communication elements.

LIVE THEATRE'S UNIQUENESS

For many, live theatrical performance manages to separate itself from similar arts and entertainment enterprises and remain special. For millions of spectators who attend live theatre in professional, community, and educational venues, there is something unique and mesmerizing about being right there with real actors. Both performers and spectators are aware that they inhabit the same or closely contiguous real space. It registers with them that they both live in the same real time and breathe the same surrounding air. To be sure, many of these same things could be said of being present at a sporting event, or a wedding, or a political rally. In the case of a live theatre performance, however, the actors and the audience share another very special pact.

In addition to having exciting real world time and space experiences in common they also share imagined experiences. They share the stuff of fictional worlds. During a live theatre performance the other-worldly energies of fictional characters are bodied forth by flesh and blood actors exclusively on the audience's behalf. Audiences are empowered by the actors and other theatre personnel to experience in *real time* the simultaneous overlay of another time, one that is other than "real" in the usual sense. Audiences also witness a readily accessible space that the performers occupy in a very special way. They see a *real place*, but one that is also coincident with another locale, an imagined one. Each theatre performance depends first of all on real world acoustical and visual triggers that enable audiences to conceive of themselves as being in two places at once. Audience members are expected to process a double dose of what can be called the *now* of experiential life.

Spectators must thus deal with a dual-leveled encounter which trumpets the fact that in the theatre two modes of experience, two kinds of event, can and do exist in the same space at the same time. This fact, although seemingly counterintuitive, nurtures the essence of theatrical magic. Much that we regard as performance magic springs from a complex experience of immediate presence. Audiences and performers are in each others' presence as both real and imagined beings. Accordingly their interaction becomes especially intense. It comes as no surprise that people who respond freely and openly to the power of mingled real and imagination-driven presence reserve an honored place in their hearts for live theatre performance. But although it exhibits an undeniable power, theatrical performance, and the crafting of it, everywhere displays its abiding fragility. That fragility shows up over and over in countless ways.

POINTS OF FRAGILITY IN THE FORMULATION AND PERCEPTION OF A PERFORMANCE

To begin with, the nascent theatrical performance is fragile at the outset, during the "making" phase. It is at this point that various collaborators, members of the performance team, actively join together, often over extended periods of time, to ready the materials and elements slated to be used in the final presentation. Each collaborator is called upon to make a specialized creative contribution to the whole which is the imagination-driven fictional world. The most capable of these collaborators carefully strive to balance their specialized contributions with those of their cohorts. They share with similarly motivated partners the goal of creating a unified and harmonious final product fueled by a kind of shared imaginative energy.

However, as in any genuine communal climate, every decision, every choice each collaborator makes inevitably has an impact, foreseen or not, on every other collaborator's contribution. The balancing act that is called for in these circumstances is always precarious and—as you probably have guessed by now—is demonstrably (and sometimes frustratingly) fragile. As a practical matter, great pains are taken to enable collaborators to communicate clearly and openly among themselves. Moreover, they continually confront the need to exercise ongoing creative flexibility, sometimes being called upon to adjust (even if it is personally painful) particular aspects of their work when special needs arise. Clearly both the exigent working conditions theatre artists and craftspeople confront as well as the stresses associated with their professional interactions foster a web that is both complex and fragile.

ARTISTIC SYNERGISM

When all the elements of a pending theatrical performance mesh harmoniously they profit from artistic synergism. Briefly defined, synergism refers to the circumstance when each collaborator's contribution works together with others in the way it should, with the strength of each effort feeding into and supporting every other effort. For an observer there are no discernible seams between the various parts or inputs. The whole enterprise is perceived to be greater than the sum of its parts. Instead of the constituent parts being readily identifiable, they merge and thus make a single integrated impression. It is then that an alternate—and magical—reality can be seen to take over, held together by the shared imaginations of the participants and executed in the presence of an appropriately responsive audience. It is important that that audience remains sensitive to the synergistic interplay of the constituent elements that make up the collaboration. When this occurs the **theatre makers** or members of the performance team have done as much as they can to urge the excellence of a performance that "works." Still, as we have already noted, the process is not complete. The crafted work needs the special act of perception which can only come from a perceptive audience.

Just as shaping and honing a pending theatrical performance can be seen as a fragile undertaking, actually executing the performance is similarly precarious. Moreover, the final step, responding to a performance, can be equally fragile and it operates at the other end of the process. This is the "perceiving" phase when discerning audiences long to be transported to a "magical" place to share the lives of the characters or the energies that motivate the characters' actions. They look forward to experiencing in vicarious fashion all that can happen in the places they imaginatively visit. But sometimes spectators find that conditions aren't precisely right. Intrusions of one kind or another can subvert their focus and inhibit their imaginations. Such interferences can easily skew a spectator's perceptions, weakening or perhaps destroying the theatrical communication (perhaps "communion" is the better word) intended by the creative artists and hoped for on the part of audiences. Sometimes these troublesome snags arise from conditions surrounding the performance. Other times, however, they exist in the minds of the audience members themselves. Prejudices, unwarranted expectations, or just plain insensitivity can inhibit appropriate spectator response and put effective theatrical communication in jeopardy. It is undoubtedly true that the theatre respondent is subject to the same pressures that affect other audience members. The principles of good spectatorship thus become very important. They form the core of the theatre respondent's power and influence.

In the face of so much fragility at both ends of the theatrical transaction it is understandable why live theatre performance does not always reach those peaks that characterize it at its best—when it is reckoned as being magical. Sometimes there is a breakdown in the crafting of the performance, and sometimes spectators are unable to tune into what has been crafted. Truly great theatre needs not only skilled artists and craftspeople to design and execute all components of the theatrical performance, it also needs open and responsive spectators who can appreciate what has been provided for them and thus effectively bring the entire creative process to a fitting conclusion. As a respondent you undertake to make this happen. You have your challenge before you.

You join teachers, artists, craftspeople, and other committed spectators who do what they can to bring about magical theatrical performance. They search for ways to make the quality of theatrical magic repeatable, to make that aura of excellence encountered in one performance or one scene carry over to the next one, and on and on. But it is uncommonly difficult to do.

THE MAGIC SMOTHERED

Sadly it often happens that when responsible and well-meaning people undertake the thoughtful consideration of live theatre, when a performance is rationally analyzed, discussed, critiqued, and evaluated, its magic, or the promise of it, can get lost. It may even be that the special synergism that characterized a transcendent theatrical experience during the time it was witnessed can get brushed aside in the subsequent discussion. It often seems to evaporate in the presence of what is often regarded as worthy critical scrutiny and when it does, one of live theatre's most attractive features is minimized. Often appraisal techniques associated with rigorous consideration of what took place, and what should take place, during a theatrical production can be at odds with theatre's evocative but elusive power.

This circumstance puts a particular strain on teachers who appraise past work and then strive to assist developing theatre artists (and even audiences) by making them aware of how they might improve in subsequent endeavors. It also frustrates the artists themselves who incessantly look for ways to recapture the aura or mystique of creative inspiration. It is no surprise to anyone that the creative process itself is notoriously subject to affective pressures that can derail the worthiest of intentions. Theatre's fragile magic, it seems, is everywhere put in jeopardy.

It is equally no surprise, then, that teachers, coaches and others who work in theatre face an ongoing challenge in trying to find ways to honor the fragile magic that characterizes theatrical performance at its best while still promoting further development based on solid analysis. Teachers and coaches especially have the burden of finding ways to witness performances and talk meaningfully about them. They have the added impetus of making each developing artist's next theatrical performance magical as well. For no one are those challenges and obligations more true than for the specialist we call the theatre respondent.

This guidebook is designed most particularly for theatre respondents or people who aspire to be respondents. It proposes a way, one way of many, but the one I happen to prefer, for them to

1. experience

2. think about, and

3. discuss theatre events

in their quest to help developing theatre artists. It outlines a sound, practical and proven approach for analyzing and evaluating performances, especially as they occur in educational and community theatres. Respondents have an unavoidable obligation. They cannot side-step the need to penetrate to the core of theatrical expressiveness. No matter how fragile the act of theatre is, respondents are called upon to confront it and communicate about it in meaningful fashion, all the while honoring whatever measure of magic arises from their witnessing the performance.

The guidebook also has much to offer people who have no desire to be formal respondents, but have an interest in the general topic of theatre spectatorship. Many teachers of any of theatre's sub-specialties as well as general audience members fall comfortably into this category.

A CAUTION

However, I want to caution you about one very important thing. This guidebook will address your sensitivity to performance, outline some useful ways you can categorize and group your responses as you communicate them to others, and it may even help you to expand your taste horizon. But it will do little to train you in the arts of theatre per se. Your prior education and experience in theatre have shaped, and will continue to shape, your artistry, your intelligence and your insights. Those are the traits that make you who you are as a theatre worker, an educator, or a spectator. What the guidebook sets out to do is to make your already functioning strengths accessible to others, to the people you seek to serve, in other words, to those many developing theatre artists who look to you, a theatre respondent, for guidance.

Though at first it may seem that viewing a theatre production appreciatively is something that can be done equally well by anyone at any time, that is not the case. Inappropriate and coarsened habits of thought have a way of intruding upon our viewing experiences in ways that deny us many of the pleasures and enlightenment that theatre can potentially offer. In other words, we are in danger of being cut off from the power and pleasure of theatre's fragile magic. Sadly, as many observers of modern culture have testified, the same kind of estranging and benumbing behaviors can and often do inhibit other parts of our living as well. The first and arguably the most important step in becoming a worthy respondent starts with work on yourself.

It also may be that this guidebook can help combat a general debilitating tendency: that is, the tendency wherein theatrical performances, and perhaps our lives, are viewed superficially and judged inappropriately. The principles set forth here undertake to sharpen the acuity of our perceptions, expand our awareness and tolerance, and cultivate our capacities for empathy—all in the context of live theatre performance. It may be that for many a suitable place to begin a larger process, one that might apply to other areas of life, is with the study and the nurturing of good theatre spectatorship skills. I optimistically cling to the hope that the precepts set forth in this guidebook, precepts that are calculated specifically to guide theatre respondents, can conceivably contribute to the start of a similar enlivening process elsewhere in our lives as well.

2

ATTENDING AND ATTENDING TO

As a theatre respondent you join with other audience members to complete the arc of theatre creativity. It is in the presence of you and your audience cohorts and with their participation (and yours) that the magic we hope for during a performance can finally happen. All the members of the performance team hold a simulacrum of all of you somewhere in their minds as they ready their contribution for your time together. But what the performance team members imagine is not always the audience they get. A theatre audience is not a simple thing.

COMPLEX AND DIVERSE AUDIENCES

Any audience at a theatrical performance is made up of individuals with varied backgrounds, theatre knowledge and personal tastes. For some of these spectators the act of attending the theatre can be regarded as a common occurrence. Others may be making it to a live presentation for the first time. Some of the people in attendance can be familiar with the production company, the script, perhaps some of the performers—they may even be friends or relatives—while others draw upon no such prior knowledge. Some have read reviews or publicity-oriented stories; others have not. Some audience members can be expected to be theatre practitioners in their own right while others have neither on-stage nor backstage experience. Some attendees have a pronounced preference for comedies or musicals while others are drawn to more somber stuff. Still others may accommodate all fare equally. Whatever their individual histories, when all these people come together in the same place at the same time they become an audience, albeit, as you probably already have realized, an interestingly mixed one. It is always intriguing to note the extent to which the diverse members of an audience seem to give up or mute aspects of their individuality in order to bond with each other to become a single entity.

People are initially motivated to attend any particular performance for diverse reasons. For example, some are looking to enhance their overall cultural awareness while others seek social interaction with other attendees. Those whose livelihoods are linked in some way to the theatre—teachers, reviewers, and fellow practitioners—actors, directors, playwrights and designers—all observe the performance with their own specific agendas in mind. However, in the overall mix of people who attend live theatre performances there is one individual who will command our interest here. That person is **you** when you assume the mantle of **theatre respondent**.

THE RESPONDENT DEFINED

As a respondent you approach the job as an outside agent, which is to say you are not a member of the immediate performance team. From your perspective as outside observer you are charged with viewing a theatre performance so as to provide meaningful responses. Following a viewing you will set forth your perceptions and experiences of the event in ways the members of the production team can find useful and illuminating. But not all who are charged with the responsibility of serving as respondents feel up to performing the job to their own and others' satisfaction. You may consider yourself to be among this sub-group. Hence the need for a guidebook which assists respondents to reflect on and prepare for what it is they undertake to do.

In some contexts respondents might be referred to as adjudicators, critics, judges, or evaluators. I prefer the term "**respondent**" because the term stresses the act of reacting to the performance over making judgments about its worth. (Of course, when things do not go well the people who perform this special task may also be characterized in other, less flattering, ways.) But whatever you and your fellow theatre respondents are called you are not to be confused with journalistic reviewers or dramaturgical critics. Although at first glance some of the observational techniques and analytic language you employ might appear to be similar, as a theatre respondent you occupy a different, but equally specialized, niche.

Part of this difference comes from the audience you will address. Your insights as a trained respondent are to be directed chiefly (but not always exclusively) to the on-site theatre workers—the artists, craftspeople, and other performance team members who made a specific live performance happen. Unlike journalistic reviewers, respondents do not set out to address a popular readership made up largely of unseen potential audiences who have not yet attended the production and are trying to decide if it will be worth their time, effort, and money. Nor is it your task to address a scholarly readership striving to place a particular production in an historical, ideological, or philosophical context. In reality, and regardless of the title you are assigned, as a respondent you will function as a hybrid between a highly focused theatre spectator and a sort of theatre teacher with a specific and limited objective. With "fresh eyes" you witness a live theatre production and then provide detailed and useful responses, coupled with performance analyses, directly to—and for the edification of—the many members of a performance team. At least that is what happens when you do your job right. Your most important task is to assist the members of the performance team, people whom you regard as developing theatre artists, to be judiciously self-aware. You are to help them survey their efforts, assess the effectiveness of those efforts, and assemble a base of knowledge and insights for use when they engage in future work.

As a theatre respondent you may perform significant collateral duties as well, but always your primary obligation is to be of service to your fellow theatre workers. Some of the other duties may be essentially administrative or bureaucratic and have their major impact in what might be called a larger operational context. For example, respondents are often relied upon to rank or evaluate productions that compete for recognition, awards, or inclusion in a future festival. Similarly, you may be asked to identify particular individuals deserving of special recognition. Evaluating, ranking, and rewarding thus become natural extensions of your primary function as a theatre respondent. But they are "extensions" and not themselves "core behaviors."

Typically you will deliver your feedback orally soon after the performance, often laboring under notably tight time constraints that affect both the preparation of your commentary and the delivery of it. In the majority of instances you will direct your comments only to a sub-set of the performance team. The sub-set usually includes the actors and director and a sprinkling of other involved parties from the pool of designers, choreographers, and technicians and others who bore some measure of responsibility for shaping the complex theatre event. While it would be beneficial if all performance team members could attend the response session that is seldom logistically possible.

However, interested fellow audience members may sometimes look on. When they do, this composite group, theatre workers and observers—all of whom participated in vastly different ways in the recent theatre event—provides you with an opportunity to enlarge the circle of your educational impact. As a respondent you are in a privileged position to help all participants plumb the essential nature of theatre, to consider how it generates social experiences, makes aesthetic meaning, and fosters humanistic understanding. For this ambitious undertaking, the immediate performance, if properly approached, serves as an illuminating case study. Helping audiences as well as practitioners reflect on the essential nature of theatre as well as its "grand purpose" writ large becomes yet another natural extension of your work as a respondent.

RESPONDENTS AS FELLOW THEATRE ARTISTS

In virtually every instance, and I assume such is true for you, respondents are transplanted theatre workers. They busily apply their insights, knowledge and talents at some venue other than the one where they function as a respondent. Your status as a practicing theatre worker creates an interesting mix of benefits and deterrents. The benefits accrue when you draw upon your practical background knowledge and experience—knowledge and experience with the "hands on" stuff—and share it meaningfully with others who feel a kind of theatre worker's kinship with you. The things you, as a practicing theatre worker, are able to focus on are likely to go to the core of what the people you are addressing hold as their principal concerns. Your well-grounded insights are likely to resonate in a special way with these people who have faced similar challenges. Under those circumstances you enjoy a positive ethos or credibility. But you must be on the alert. Problems can arise if any respondent's personal artistic preferences, which may be highly individualized and passionately embraced, interfere with a fair and objective viewing of a particular production team's alternate approach and interpretation. In other words, a particular commitment to the way you might have produced the show can blind you to what has been put before you. In those instances any respondent who ignores the perspectives of the present production by insisting on personal preferences is quite likely to be marginalized in the minds of the listeners, perhaps even actively rejected and charged with unwarranted bias.

Functioning at their best, however, theatre respondents work hard to purge (or at least minimize) their biases and personal preferences. They work to be knowledgeable, responsible and open-minded witnesses of a production. They communicate useful impressions and insights that benefit their fellow theatre workers. They do not re-direct or re-design or rewrite or pointedly revise the existing show. And yet one of your strengths as a respondent will lie in the fact that you bring fresh eyes and a new perspective to the creative work of people who, in their own way and in their own circumstances, behave much like you do when, on your home turf, you too craft theatrical performances. As such a respondent you occupy a special place of considerable value.

However a subtle but related danger can, on occasion, undermine the value of the response process. A popular respondent, wittingly or unwittingly, may end up cloaked in a kind of presumptive authority. The implied power that comes with that cloaking, even when it is unsought, can be seductive and potentially counterproductive. It can lead the respondent to overreach, to take oneself too seriously, and offer "directives and prescriptions" when "responses and descriptions" are in order. As a respondent your task, properly addressed, is neither to speak from "on high" nor to amass personal power. It is to *empower others* to be more effective theatre artists in their future endeavors. This simple objective, though easily stated, calls for humility and selflessness of a high order. In the final analysis, you should recognize that the real power and responsibility for actual change properly belongs in the hands of the on-site practicing artists rather than with you or any other visiting respondent.

ASSUMPTIONS ABOUT THEATRE EVENTS

You, like every other respondent, every other audience member, indeed like every theatre worker, undoubtedly have mental images of what a theatre event is, how it operates, and what it seeks to do. However, the details of these mental images typically remain unarticulated. They lurk below the level of conscious awareness. They are easily taken for granted. From this secure and private zone these images inform the ways theatre workers, respondents and general audience members view and think about any theatre event. In effect they constitute a private mental grid or index of reference points (some might call it a template or a paradigm) against which the entire theatre event, any theatre event, is viewed.

Each individual's template also implies the standards by which aspects of an event are ultimately adjudged appropriate and effective. At the outer edge, a person's template even dictates what kind of activity qualifies to be called a theatre event. Not surprisingly, perhaps, there can be marked disagreement among observers who presume to judge the same theatre events. After all, each person potentially is free to draw upon the parameters of a privately held template. But, thankfully, in practice it is not always as chaotic as this brief description might make it seem.

Templates held by different people need not, and very often do not, differ drastically from one another. The bulk of them are forged from commonly held assumptions and beliefs that respondents and general audience members share whether they know it or not. Shared assumptions and beliefs grow out of, and help perpetuate, a community's doctrine of taste and values. It is only when tastes and values are not fully shared that a community's judgments can be fractured with the result that competing doctrines get put forth.

Alternative standards typically derive from an individual's unique experience of cultural or sub-cultural encounters. Such things as generational differences, religious differences, political differences, divergent past theatre experiences, all contribute to the shaping of people's differing templates. And the list of influences does not stop there. But underlying all the divergent preferences and the virtually unlimited varieties of theatrical expressiveness are the theatre event and the theatrical performance's root traits. If you keep these traits in mind you will be guided in ways that will help you in your encounters with both familiar and unfamiliar performance styles.

THE EMPIRICAL PERFORMANCE

At its elemental and sub-verbal level, the theatrical performance you confront is a visual and acoustic event that unfolds during the passage of time and within a prescribed space. Every part of it is the product of some person's or group's choice, whether that choice is active (intended) or passive (accidental or unintended).

THE PERFORMANCE IMAGE

The performance embodies an image of an alternate reality. That image is of a fictional (fictive) world. Your perception of it results from your interaction with the **performance text**, that multi-faceted stimulus painstakingly created by all the members of the production company. Taken as a whole, the core performance team is populated by numerous collaborators, both artists and craftspeople, who select, shape, and execute the constituent parts of the performance text. Also worth a measure of your attention are the people who facilitate the performance as a whole, but from a place somewhere outside the obvious workings of the fictional world. I have in mind the anonymous (and often unseen) technicians and crew members, including ushers and box office personnel, who typically disappear from audience consciousness, at least until they make an intrusive error that has a negative impact. On those occasions they are likely to be reviled.

The fictive world that is intentionally cued into our consciousness by the performance text ultimately exists only as a perception. What is magic about it—its unique theatrical nature and the wellspring of its fragile magic—thus qualifies as an **illusion**. But that perceived fictive world, that theatrical illusion, has the potential power to provoke real world consequences. Moreover, it is certainly brought into being by the manipulation of materials and behaviors that clearly can be seen to have a non-fictional and real world dimension

When you deliver your commentary to the production company you will refer to the fictive world delineated by your interaction with the performance. In personal terms that fictive world is the one you perceived, experienced, and remember. In the practical terms of perception, any parts of it you didn't see or hear—for any reason—do not exist for you. Your consequent experience is derived from your perception, limited or full, of the fictive world. Typically you trust it to be a reliable measure of the evocative power of the performance text. Since your actual commentary occurs after the performance is completed, your memories of the performance text, the fictive world it suggested, and the experience you underwent are all the things you can actually draw upon to fuel your discussion.

PREPARING TO WITNESS THE PERFORMANCE

The act of witnessing a theatrical performance by both general spectators and respondents proceeds in the same way, or at least it ideally ought to. In ideal terms both groups attempt to make themselves psychologically and emotionally available to the simulation of life embodied in the performance. They empty their minds of everything that might be extraneous or distracting so as to allow the performance to fully capture their imaginations.

Obviously while this is an easy thing to say, it is not always an easy thing to do, since expectations, assumptions, and other distracting thoughts are abundant. But in order to fulfill your function as respondent and to fully experience the imagination-driven content of the performance you should make yourself open to the nuances of its operation. You should free your mind to accept, for the duration of the performance, the illusion of life being depicted and the implications it suggests. In other words, you focus maximum attention on the fictive world and all that is contained therein. You actively will yourself to believe, for the time being, the imagination-driven acts and incidents put before you. For the duration of the performance you put faith in the existence of the characters and their motivations. At the same time you will always know, in another part of your brain, that the characters and motivations you are witnessing are make-believe. You certainly recognize that the actors depicting them are real.

For a host of reasons, some of which are suggested above, not everyone is equally adept at doing this, at "going along with" the guidance provided by the performance. For example, rigid adherence to particular templates can lead some audience members to make exclusionary judgments. That is, those performance traits not aligned with an observer's existing templates can be rejected or at least found wanting. When the general spectator does this it constitutes an exercise, understandable and perhaps excusable, of personal taste and preference. The theatre respondent, however, operates in a different context and faces a specialized set of obligations. As part of your covenant as a theatre respondent you are obliged, to the best of your abilities and for the duration of the performance, to embrace whatever vision animates the performance text. You do this in order to subsequently judge its worth and internal consistency—two of the criteria that most interest developing theatre artists. This guidebook is dedicated to helping you take the practical steps to make that happen in a way that will nurture theatre's fragile magic.

3

THE THEATRE EVENT'S PARA-AESTHETIC COMPONENT

COMPONENTS OF THE THEATRE EVENT

The practical reality that a respondent faces is that every theatre performance is inevitably embedded in a larger event. That larger event, which we can conveniently call the **theatre event**, divides naturally into two component parts. One is the performance per se, the complex crafted artifact that all the collaborators, artists and craftspeople, labor to bring into being. It constitutes the aesthetic component of the theatre event. The other component is all the rest of what surrounds the central aesthetic portion. It is the **para-aesthetic component**.

Of the two, it is the aesthetic component that is most readily identified and focused on—sometimes to the exclusion of all else. Not surprisingly, it is also the aesthetic component of a theatre event that commands almost all of the respondent's (and the spectator's) conscious attention. Also, not surprisingly, it elicits the bulk of their commentaries. However, the quality of their attention and the perceptiveness of their commentaries are influenced, often to a surprising degree, by the conditioning effects of the other, less obvious, part of the theatre event, its para-aesthetic component. As a respondent it behooves you to take all of this into account.

PARA-AESTHETICS

The dominant forces that shape a theatre event's para-aesthetic nature are typically driven by "real world" or "social" concerns. This distinction separates them, generally speaking, from the creative and imaginative concerns of the theatre artists and craftspeople whose efforts are focused on conceiving and shaping the event's aesthetic component, what we refer to as the **performance text**. The performance text remains the primary

21

aesthetic artifact of interest to the respondent and most of the members of the production team. It is the performance text that displays the fictional (or fictive) world, the "pretend world" specifically designed to be accessed by an audience's imagination.

Nonetheless, it is important that you recognize that the clusters of conditions surrounding and framing the performance remain important even though they may be passed over in typical discussions of the performance *per se*. You as a respondent, like the general audience members, cannot avoid being affected by the para-aesthetic components of any theatre event you attend (and attend to). In practice these two aspects of the theatre event may blend together or overlap in such a way as to blur casual perception. It is useful for any aspiring respondent to consider them separately in order to become aware of their influential powers. Chronologically the para-aesthetic stimuli are the first to influence auditors.

In the process of focusing their attention on that fictive world many people either ignore or take the para-aesthetic dimensions of a theatre event for granted—at least, that is, until some malfunctioning para-aesthetic element creates distractions or discomfort. But even when para-aesthetic features go by unmentioned and elude our conscious awareness they are capable of exercising considerable, albeit often subtle, influences on the way the aesthetic component of the theatre event—the performance *per se*—is perceived and appreciated.

Many para-aesthetic aspects associated with a theatre event are directly linked to its physical environment. They include such seemingly mundane things as the comfort and arrangement of the seats (if there are seats), the temperature of the audience space (is it excessively hot or cold?), the quality of the air (does it smell stale? smoky? fresh?), the ambient noise level (does sound bleed through from adjacent spaces? From outside? Is the air handling system noisy or quiet?), the acoustics that determine how easy it is to hear and understand the performers (does the sound reverberate so as to blur clear perception? Is it muffled by surfaces that deaden the sound and "swallow it up?" Are the sounds crisp and easy to understand?), the general light level (can audience members see to get to their seats easily? Can they read their programs? Are the exits clearly visible?) and uncounted other influences of a similar nature.

Within obvious limits, many physical environment stimuli are viewed as the "givens" of the performance space. They simply seem to be there, unchanging and constant. But often members of the production team manage to modify them. When they do, they undertake to create a climate for the audience, a surrounding context that hopefully contributes in some way to the apt viewing of the performance. Putting ushers in costumes that echo the fictive world is one such technique. Decorating the auditorium space so as to create an environment that blends with the fictive space of the play is another.

Para-aesthetic elements are significant in large measure because many of them affect directly the feelings of safety and comfort that you and the others in attendance, experience. A shaky seating platform or a broken seat can so worry any patron that little else is attended to during the course of the performance. A malfunctioning air handling system, one that keeps the room at too high a temperature or one that is so noisy as to make it difficult to hear easily, can create a distraction that is difficult if not impossible to overcome. With this in mind it is easy to see how para-aesthetic influences help to create the ambiance, set the stage, so to speak, for the way audience members relax (or find it difficult to relax) into the fictive world of the performance. When the para-aesthetic features of the theatre event shield the patron from distraction or discomfort they serve to empower and enhance the spectators' individual and collective imaginations. In sum, they exert a subtle but pervasive power to help—or, alternatively, to hinder—the way auditors partake of the aesthetic experience offered them by the production.

Understandably front-of-house theatre workers, operating in ways that are similar in many respects to the physical environment, are in a position to influence greatly each theatregoer's para-aesthetic encounter with the theatre event. The relative efficiency and friendliness of box office personnel, for example, do much to shape an audience member's mood. The ushers, too, have a discernible influence (do they greet audience members appropriately? Do they guide them to their proper seats? Are they appropriately attentive to people needing special assistance?). The front-of-house workers typically make the first contact with audience members approaching and entering the theatre event site. When they do their jobs well they do not intrude unduly into the audience's consciousness. When they deflect the audience's attention from the impending performance they act to inhibit, either greatly or slightly, the dynamics of the aesthetic transaction.

Even members of the audience in attendance wield para-aesthetic influence, either subtly or boldly. This becomes most evident when audience-based distractions occur. For example, an enthusiastic and noisy theatre party within a larger gathering clearly creates an atmosphere that affects the others that surround them. Conversely, a subdued and respectful audience core can create an atmosphere that encourages others to follow their lead. Certainly beeping watches or pagers, crying children, talking or coughing patrons, and the like can interfere mightily with an audience's ability to concentrate. Even the presence of a celebrity in the house can skew the focus and receptivity of an audience in significant ways.

Of course, theatre events provide ample opportunities for social interaction. For a great many people one of the biggest pleasures of attending live theatre is allied to its social nature. The potency of any theatrical experience is likely to be enhanced when the reactive aesthetic experience is a shared communal one. As individuals we laugh more easily when others laugh. We cry when others cry. We get the point of a confrontation between characters when others react to it as well. Fellow audience members help us all focus our attention. An audience is made up of individuals, but at the same time it becomes an identifiable entity unto itself. Although social interactions and behaviors are para-aesthetic in their essential nature, they have a profound influence on the audience's perception of a theatre event's aesthetic contribution.

Any listing of influential para-aesthetic stimuli can extend well beyond the confines of the performance space itself. A patron's ease in simply locating a particular theatre during a first time visit is just such a factor. So, too, are such things as the proximity of acceptable parking, the lighting on foot pathways, the ease of access for the handicapped, and the like. Even the posters and ads that advertise the production and the program that announces the performers and describe the settings and action play a part in shaping expectations. However, these latter elements qualify as special instances of para-aesthetic influence. They are special because they are readily recognized by all who view them to be directly linked to and therefore legitimate extensions of the event's aesthetic component.

Other features of a performance can derive from para-aesthetic concerns that dovetail neatly into practical aesthetic needs. When a performance has intermissions or the need for time to effect changes of costume, scenery or props between scenes the flow of the production is naturally affected. Even an ill-timed delay between the time the house lights go down and the curtain goes up to begin the action can influence an audience member's receptivity. In festival situations the set-up and strike of a show can be a potent para-aesthetic element.

The list of potential para-aesthetic elements could go on and on. Assessing their relative power is not always easy, except perhaps when they trigger undesirable reactions. But, whether they are seen as positive or negative, they always have the power to influence the audience's interaction with a theatrical event. It is for this reason that they deserve your thoughtful attention and in many cases a focused comment.

PARA-AESTHETIC EFFECTS

The sum effect of all the various para-aesthetic features of a theatre event is that they condition the reactions of audience members and the respondent in subtle but telling ways. Being aware of them is the first step you must take in order to urge theatre workers to exercise "real world" and "social" controls in ways that that enhance—or at least do not distract from—a performance's aesthetic influence. Here, too, you are in a privileged position to guide all the theatre workers to be alert to those para-aesthetic forces that have such telling influence on effective theatre spectatorship.

THE RESPONDENT AND PARA-AESTHETICS

Anyone who has participated in the shaping of a theatre event knows that at every step in its evolution it flirts with unlocking or, alternatively, muting its fragile magic power. Producing a theatre event is a complex undertaking. Innumerable decisions are made by a host of collaborators as they work over considerable time to fully craft it. Many things, some foreseeable, others unpredictable, can go awry. When they do, the audience's eventual appreciation of the theatre event is put in jeopardy. In practical terms you, functioning as an effective respondent, should learn to identify and mentally isolate those para-aesthetic distractions that would otherwise skew your aesthetic response. Then, in order to help the theatre artists and craftspeople shape apt and powerful theatre events in the future, you are in a position to guide them to a heightened awareness of the pervasive effects, both positive and negative, of para-aesthetic stimuli.

4

THE THEATRE EVENT'S
AESTHETIC COMPONENT

The production (or performance) *per se* is by far the theatre event's more important component. It is the event's aesthetic component. Understandably it is the performance that (especially when it "works") commands the closest attention of any audience. The more clearly you as a respondent witness it, the more it emerges as a many-faceted and many-tiered stimulus, one that both elicits and structures an audience's willing response. Barring pesky overpowering para-aesthetic distractions it is the key determinant of every observer's theatrical experience. Though the aesthetic component of a theatre event may frequently seem disarmingly simple and direct, it is not. When you consider closely how it is formed, how it functions in the transaction that we call theatre viewing, and how it is typically perceived it turns out to be complex, often difficult to discuss, and always surprisingly fragile. Surely your time spent in theatre has already acquainted you with key aspects of its overall functioning, but reflecting on them one more time can still prove useful. If, as a respondent, you really understand the bases upon which a performance rests you are more likely to guide others to a fuller appreciation of their tasks and responsibilities as theatre artists and craftspeople.

COLLABORATION FOR PERCEPTION

Putting together a theatre performance is a collaborative enterprise, a fact everyone who writes about or practices theatre readily admits. It is an enterprise, involving many workers, that is calculated to create a carefully modulated or shaped illusion. When all its facets, all the contributory threads, are taken into account, the eventual performance can only be reckoned as extremely complex. This fact makes your task of characterizing it in words surprisingly elusive. Its complex nature bears tacit witness to many peoples' imaginations at work. From the earliest stirrings of the collaborators' efforts to shape it, each performance is inevitably bent toward an audience's perception. Theatrical performance, put quite simply, is designed to be witnessed. In fact, it can be argued—rather convincingly, in my opinion—that whatever the skilled processes are that go into the making of a theatrical performance, it is not truly a work of **theatre art** until it is witnessed by an audience. It certainly has not achieved the end toward which it was directed until that eventuality has been reached.

THE COLLABORATORS

Various theatre artists and craftspeople (e.g. playwrights, composers, directors, designers, actors, scenic and costume technicians, lighting and sound board operators, etc.) employ a wide array of means to project a complex illusion that, for the duration of the performance, is intended to substitute for, or at least dominate, all other views of the world. The "stuff" of the performance text sets forth an alternate reality or fictive world. That world, apparent to the observers, is illusory in the sense that it is wholly in the service of a guiding artistic vision; it is an act of integrated imagination. As has already been noted and you surely have long recognized, theatre in its essential state always depends on the human ability to "make believe," both in the creative "making phase" and in the "perceiving phase." That double circumstance, though fundamental to the essential aesthetic portion of a theatre event, can sometimes be forgotten. Both creators and spectators—respondents included—are called upon to exercise and to monitor their imaginative faculties. When either of those tasks is neglected, faulty standards of judgment are often the result.

THE SPECTATOR'S CHALLENGE

Every theatre performance challenges all who witness it to set aside habitual beliefs and modes of perception in order to imaginatively enter into whatever fictive world it sets forth. In other words, it calls for us as audience members (and especially as respondents) to willingly and obligingly suspend (set aside) our tendency to disbelieve or discount fiction. We do so in order to set our imaginations free to be employed in the final act of creating theatre. We are the responsive agents who play out in our minds and imaginations the life that animates the fictive world stimulated by the performance text. The final locus of the all-important theatre image, the one provoked by the performance text, is in the minds of the spectators. It is thus the spectators who perform that final creative (or, if you prefer, that "empowering") act. Doing so in an equitable way is a challenge, a challenge which takes us down many avenues worth considering if we wish to be effective respondents. Because the overall enterprise of theatre presents so many diverse faces, a strong measure of imaginative flexibility is called for if any specific performance is to be viewed effectively on its own terms.

THEATRE'S MANY FACES

Sometimes the faces of theatre are so different from one another it is difficult to see them all as belonging to the same kind of enterprise. Sometimes the various contributing elements of the artistically created illusion closely resemble the world around us; other times they are wildly different from anything we are likely to see in "real life." Always, however, what appears in the fictive world is an abstraction shaped by the many makers of the theatrical illusion. It is an abstraction if for no other reason than that it is a construct with some details omitted and other details highlighted. Sometimes we are lulled into forgetting that.

The behaviors and happenings within the alternate reality often can be precise and painstakingly detailed or, alternatively, they can be generalized through stylization and suggestion. Whether rendered in close detail or in broad sweeping strokes they frame and reveal the **fictive world**'s essential existence.

The substitute universe set forth in the performance may actively invite an audience's participation, real or vicarious. On the other hand it may strive to keep its observers at a psychological and physical distance. Empathizing with a character takes spectators psychologically closer to that character's experience. Being denied access to signs of a character's "inner life" encourages witnesses to see that character as an unknowable force, or a "type," or part of a faceless crowd. When a performer addresses patrons directly, or perhaps physically invades the audience's space, the dynamic nature of spectator/character involvement is undoubtedly different from that called for when the fictive world operates with no open acknowledgment of the spectator's presence.

On some occasions the fictive world set forth by the performance text may encourage the spectators' measured and somber intellectual contemplation, perhaps even calling upon them to reflect thoughtfully on weighty issues that smack of philosophical or political meaning. At other times audiences may be so bombarded with whirlwinds of sensory stimuli that they are catapulted into focusing almost exclusively on immediate visceral responses with little opportunity left for intellectual reflection.

THE VARIABLE NATURE OF THEATRICAL PERFORMANCE

As you can readily see, that which we call "theatre performance" embraces a wide variety of goals and means. But whatever form it takes, whatever strategies are employed, whatever specialized practices are called into play, the aesthetic component of the theatre event is always a constructed and artful version of an imagined reality no matter how seemingly recognizable or strange it may appear, no matter how apparently complete or suggestive it may be bodied forth, no matter how emotionally alluring or forbidding is its impact. Theatrical performance exists as the imaginative embodiment of an illusory world, a world rendered in "real" terms, which many workers, working together, design and execute just for human perception. It is "real" in the sense that, within the parameters of our responsive imagination, it occurs in real time, in real space, using real world materials, focusing on the supposedly real behaviors of what seem for the moment to be real people, even though all of this is the expression of the combined imaginations of the collaborating theatre artists who shaped it.

PERFORMANCE TEXT

The designation "performance text" is the convenient name we have chosen to identify the complex, both verbal and non-verbal, stimuli the many theatre collaborators select, craft, and place before audiences. It is the performance text that sets forth, in palpable "real world" manifestations, the fictive world each audience perceives. It is the temporal and spatial "text" that audiences "read" when they process a performance's visual and auditory stimuli. In this way they bear witness to the theatrical illusion that is unfolding before them. It sometimes proves unfortunate that everything that is perceptible during a performance, both the intended and the unintended elements, contribute to (or, at the very least, influence) audience members' responses. As a consequence it can be difficult, even for you as a trained respondent, to determine with certainty which of the features are legitimate parts of the artists' intentional performance text and which are accidents. In either case, it is the complex performance text—as perceived by the audience—that embodies the image of a fictive world and fuels each audience member's reactive imagination.

As you undoubtedly recognize, the complexity of a performance text derives, in part, from the way it comes into being. It is assembled by many people, each of them executing specialized tasks, over an extended period of time. In the complex performance that finally is presented for public consumption you, as a specially trained audience member, encounter a multitude of carefully honed stimuli, all designed to conjure up some aspect of the fictive world.

The complexity of the performance text also results, in large measure, from the way all those perceived elements intermingle and influence one another. For example, it is not only the particular words the character says that shape the audience's perceptions; it is the way they are delivered. It is not only the color, cut, style and identifiable period of any costumes worn that is important, but also how they fit the body of the performer, whether pressed or rumpled, and how the performer manipulates them. It is not only the stimulus/response patterns displayed by the characters as they interact, but also how rapidly and authoritatively such interactions occur and how confident the characters appear to be. It is not only the selection of furniture present onstage but also the degree to which each piece is precisely rendered or, at the other end of the continuum, abstractly suggested. In other words, it is both the identifiable "thing" and the execution of the "thing" that are meaningful.

It can easily be acknowledged that in a performance the impact of "**execution**" often outstrips the evocative power of the "object" or "verbiage" being executed. In these cases, it is the manner of execution that can carry the intended communicative freight. For example, the two words "you devil" can be sinister, sexy, cajoling, threatening, evidence of a horrifying realization, or the sign of a sudden glorious insight, simply by the way the three syllables are delivered and how they are heard in conjunction with accompanying physical gestures. And that example merely scratches the surface of the many possibilities that can be set in motion by an actor's painstakingly shaped behavior. If you will reflect for a moment on your past experience as a theatre worker you will be able to list a dizzying array of your own examples of this principle in action.

Identifiable patterns among seemingly discrete production elements also contribute to the performance text's complexity. To be sure, many of these patterns can be traced back to the script that informs the production, but they are truly most perceptible within the life of the performance, during its enactment. For example, a conflict that arises between a father and his son in one scene can be echoed or contrasted with the perceived relations between another father and son in a different scene. The actual physical placement of the two scenes on the stage as well as the tenor of the individual participants' energies as they engage in conflict actively control an audience's imaginative involvement, hence the aesthetic perception. (Such a patterned repetition gives rise to the identification of a motif.) Think of the script of *King Lear* and then immediately think of any production of the show you have seen.

A protagonist's apparent rise in worldly fortunes might well be accompanied by a contrasting decline in that character's general happiness and well-being. Here the embodiment of those qualities through costuming and actor-driven behaviors echo and extend anything that can be found in the page-bound script. Of course, the story of *Macbeth* could suggest such an arc, but be sure to refer in your mind to a live performance of the play as well as to the script itself.

The arc of a character's life story can be seen to parallel, or be set in an interesting juxtaposition to, the changing circumstances of an estate, or a town, or a country. Certainly *The Cherry Orchard* and productions of it reference just such a pattern. The contrasts in costume, setting, lighting, and the distribution of props between the early moments of a performance and its closing moments likely provide auditors with non-verbal cues that stimulate much of the relevant aesthetic experience.

Non-verbal linkages also provide patterns. In all performances the shared colors of costumes can subtly link compatible characters to one another or, alternatively, contrasting colors can set characters in opposition as apparent adversaries. The intensity and coloration of lights in a scene can provide clues suggesting a character's mental state through the use of sensory data that imaginatively reflects that character's inner emotional life. The intensity of lights can also guide an audience's attention and direct focus toward other elements that are to be compared and contrasted. The possibilities for observable patterns within the texture of a performance are abundant. In fact, they seem almost limitless. These patterns invite an audience—and especially you, the respondent—to consider deeper implications of the fictive world's texture and its evocative power as you witness its stage-worthy elements.

THE EVER-CHANGING "NOW"

The performance text, in addition to being a juxtaposed array of its constituent parts which form complex patterns deserving of extended interpretation, is an artifact that remains especially elusive for another significant reason. Stated simply, this is because it is **always changing** as it unfolds in time. Theatre performance is a time-based art; change is part of its fundamental nature. It is worth remembering that the whole performance text is **never** present in its entirety at any given point in time. It is always "now" as we view a performance, but each "now" gives way to the next "now," and the next, and so on. Moreover, unlike films that can be rewound and played again, videos which can be reversed or fast-forwarded, books which can be thumbed through in either direction, live theatrical performance unfolds in one direction only and it does so at enactment speed. The responsible observer, whether respondent or regular audience member, is obligated to attend to, and remember, what is happening moment by moment just to stay abreast of the ever-shifting events. In this respect, too, live theatrical performance is hauntingly like real life. As with our lives, theatrical performance unfolds inexorably toward an end, a conclusion which cannot be known with certainty until the precise moment it has arrived.

It is sometimes difficult to deal with the mercurial now. This is not to say that an audience member or a respondent cannot reflect on what has already happened and link those reflections to speculations as to what might yet occur, but even such reflections and speculations cannot remain static. They must be continually revised in the face of newly perceived data that stream by inexorably and without convenient pause. If the makers of the performance text and the witnesses of the performance text are in sync, all is well and the fictive world can be freely and fully experienced. But if either group limps unduly or lurches forward in an uncontrolled or unsubstantiated fashion dissonance results. No matter how it proceeds, it is only after the performance is completed that the spectator has personal access to all the data that can inform meaning, and that body of data is only in the form of memory, memory that has been shaped by, and is subject to, the quality of the auditor's moment-by-moment perceptions.

PERFORMANCE TEXT AND WRITTEN SCRIPT

The performance text has another important, and often controversial, characteristic which, in particular circumstances, you may be called upon to consider. It has to do with the relationship the performance text as performed bears to the script as written. Among the issues at stake are how faithfully the performance text represents the characters, dialogue, situations, thought processes, and emotional tenor of the written play. (Obviously this kind of consideration applies only to productions based on a written script rather than those deriving from a topic or situation used to prompt performers' improvisations.) Assessing faithfulness to the playwright's original intent and compositional means calls for a comparison of the written script, or to be more precise, particular interpretations of the written script, with the performance text. But that is not always an easy thing to do. In part that is because every theatrical production based on a written text is at heart a transmutation, a different order of being. Rather than the performance being a "translation" of the written script it is more like a "transliteration." It represents a crossover from one medium to another. That is, what is rendered in the medium of the printed text by means of words on the page is re-rendered in the time/space medium of theatre by means of such things as live performers, spoken speech with all of its aural characteristics, gestures, costumes, lights, sound effects, and all the other accoutrements associated with performance. Direct comparison of the two is awkward at best. The respondent undertaking such comparisons must resort to using a third intellectual space as a kind of shared currency that provides common access to both. What then can be compared in the field of "shared currency" is the body of impressions generated in the mind of the reader/auditor both from reading the script and from viewing the performance. Even then, however, there is plenty of room for slippage. For example, though the same dialogue of words may exist in both media, only one has vocal timbre, pitch, and inflectional patterning attached. An imagined character, even if described in painstaking detail in the written text, is replaced in the theatre by a living being with bulk, behavioral tics, and other individualizing traits that spark the auditor's imagination and responses in ways that are categorically different from those provoked by reading words. Add to all of this the fact that a director (or in some cases a producer or some other influential shaper of the theatre event) is likely to put forth a particularized interpretation of the written script, one that can reshape many of the constituent elements.

Interpretation, or, alternatively, the guiding vision that shapes the performance text through its linkage to the written script, is a process best seen as falling somewhere on a lengthy continuum. At one end of the continuum lies the precise and detailed execution of the playwright's compositional efforts. In this instance all dialogue is preserved, word for word. All characters are rendered as accurate representations of their written counterparts insofar as age, gender, race, and other demographic traits are concerned. The sequence of scenes is the same on the stage as it was on the page. No incidents or events are interpolated that are not indicated in the written text. Such a performance is usually adjudged to be "faithful" to the script.

Playwrights or their estates often invoke strong legal pronouncements to insure that nothing is changed from the original script in the rendering of the performance text. Indeed, so strong is the desire for textual fidelity (which is often expanded to include the somewhat problematic concept of "author's intent") that sometimes productions have been shut down.

For example, a production of Samuel Beckett's *Endgame* ran afoul of the administrators of Beckett's estate because the production decision was made to set the play in a post-apocalyptic subway. Playwright Edward Albee has objected to cross-gender casting in *Who's Afraid Of Virginia Woolf?* The Rodgers and Hammerstein leasing agency closed a production of *Big River* because of cross-racial casting wherein Jim was Caucasian and Huck was African-American. Arthur Miller prohibited the use of portions of one of his plays in a production by an experimental theatre group. All these examples clearly illustrate how legal constraints can be invoked to preserve the primacy of the written script as it is incorporated into a performance script.

Progressing step by step toward the other end of the interpretation continuum are those performance texts conceived with what most observers consider as minor alterations. These gradually shade into performances that are more extensively reworked. Sometimes the reworking is dictated by the exigencies of the production circumstances. For example, a production being considered for a festival showing may be restricted as to running time. If a cutting or adaptation of a full-length script is forged so as to meet, let us say, a one-hour playing time there is an inevitable reworking of the original text.

Sometimes the reworking of a script, whether minor or extensive, may also result from immediate casting constraints. A peripheral role originally designated as a male role may be converted to a female role, often without a significant impact on the overall production. Some directors might be compelled to eliminate nudity from their productions in deference to the sensibilities of particular performers, or perhaps to avoid offending prospective audience members. Similarly directors may modify strong language they fear their audiences may find unwarranted, or they may eliminate on-stage smoking or modify instances of on-stage drinking or other behaviors that they do not consider to be crucial to the central action. Directors often modernize archaic language so as to facilitate easy understanding. While any of these modifications of the original script technically may qualify as violations in a legal sense, in practice they are usually treated as acceptable alterations with the proviso that they are guided by ethical concerns for maintaining the author's central intent.

As noted earlier, however, the author's intent is difficult to discern with certainty. Often directors make rather extensive changes to the written script and still do so claiming to be advancing the author's intent. Those same changes can easily strike someone else as beyond the pale and thus they can be viewed as unethical alterations. Consequently, there are, in the wide-ranging mid-section of the interpretation continuum, many instances that can be hotly debated and variously argued. If we add to the mix a director's or producer's desire to create a performance text to capture a particular historical work in a way that preserves an historical aura the issue of "fidelity" gets even more complicated.

Imagining some possible performance texts for Shakespeare's *Julius Caesar* that purport to accommodate historical perspectives can serve to illustrate how issues have to be considered even when history is used as a guide. Even if we obligingly put aside the idea of young men playing women's roles as happened in Shakespeare's time, accept standard modern practices regarding performance in an auditorium with seats for everyone in the audience, and admit the use of artificial stage lighting we find directors still face important choices. For purposes of brief illustration, let's restrict our focus here to the issue of costuming.

When undertaking the staging of Shakespeare's *Julius Caesar* the performance's chief decision-makers must consider whether or not the performers are to be costumed in Roman garb reflective of the period in which the play's action takes place. Such a choice might suggest a harmony between known historical events and the characters' dress. However, the choice might also be made to dress actors in garments reflective of Shakespeare's time when the play was originally staged, thus capturing a sense of the period of the play's composition. Historical evidence suggests that the original staging of that time may well have featured actors wearing clothing of their own period supplemented with suggestive overlays of Roman garments. Does that then allow for actors of our time to wear today's garments augmented by Roman clothing elements, thus replicating the kind of "time collapsing" viewing experience the audiences of Shakespeare's time enjoyed? Credible arguments can be advanced for any of these options, and even more possibilities lie in translating the play's action to a more modern period wherein social issues seen to be comparable to those of the fictive world are evoked by the costuming choices. The celebrated Mercury Theatre production that invoked thoughts about the growth of fascism just prior to World War II by costuming its central characters in dark trench coats employed just such a rationale.

PENETRATING THE GUIDING THOUGHT

A key point to derive from these examples, and one you as respondent would do well to keep in mind, is that there are many legitimate ways, some unforeseen by the audience members, to shape a performance text. It is part of every respondent's task to penetrate the aggregated specific theatrical practices in order to illumine the thought that informed each of the various creative choices. What you seek as respondent is a sense of the inner life of the performance text as displayed in the pattern of its collaborators' decisions. Obviously this requires the respondent to set aside particular, and perhaps countervailing, expectations so as to allow the artistic collaborators' conception of the specific performance text to exercise its full influence.

OTHER THAN SCRIPT BASES FOR PERFORMANCE

Not all theatre performances derive from the energies contained in a written text that persists as some sort of touchstone for the performance staging. Some performance texts considered more radical crowd into the furthest reaches of the interpretation continuum. They gain their vitality principally from conditions that are extrinsic to the script. Accordingly, they may set forth fictive worlds with traits that cannot easily—if at all—be verified in any pre-existing scripts. Such extensive reworking of the script is usually based on a psychological or societal model that may originally have been suggested by some feature or reference discernible in the written text. It may equally be based on a social critique the director wishes to put forward using a written text as a convenient reference point. For example, the complexities and cross currents of a character's psychological makeup can be represented by multiple actors appearing simultaneously as that single character. Similarly, hearing-impaired actors can join with hearing-capable actors in performances wherein shadow performers match audible dialog with complementary signed speech. Actors can also be employed to portray multiple characters in an ever-changing fluid fashion. Dialogue can be changed to incorporate references from popular culture. In all of these instances arguments about the ethics and aesthetic validity of such productions abound. But, personal convictions, legal injunctions, and stylistic preferences aside, such productions can and do exist and you are likely to confront them. While functioning as a respondent you must find a way to deal with them equitably in order to serve the needs of the developing artists. The developing artists remain your primary concern.

SPECTATOR OBLIGATIONS

A conscientious respondent (or audience member) must be sensitive and open to whatever kind of performance text is presented. It is not an easy task to set aside personal tastes and preferences, especially when an assessment is expected at some point in the response transaction. But that is precisely what a theatre respondent endeavors to do. As response opportunities accumulate over time the respondent can cultivate personal ways to effectively encounter a performance so as to amass the data needed for an equitable response. But such self-teaching is never completely easy. It requires the exercise of theatre intelligence, intellectual discipline and a spirit of personal selflessness. The pattern of the formal response delivered to the performance team reveals and replicates the nature of the experience the respondent undergoes while witnessing the performance. A consideration of it can guide us.

5

DESCRIPTION

GETTING UNDER WAY

When the performance is over, you, as performance respondent, assume a much more active role. Throughout the performance the team members have laid their work before you. It now becomes your task to provide a commentary which will make clear to them the observations, insights, and appraisals that their efforts have stimulated in you. It is worth reminding yourself that you always do this on their behalf. Your ultimate goal is to help them understand how theatre generates meaningful and valuable experiences—particularly its fragile magic—and how they might improve their ability to contribute to that complex enterprise. In what can conceivably be an emotionally charged atmosphere immediately following a performance, *how* you say what you say to the members of the performance team can prove to be crucial.

One of the practical challenges you face as a performance respondent is to quickly organize your thoughts for your commentary. Typically the oral response to a performance is delivered very soon after that performance is completed. Utilizing an organizational plan whereby you can group useful information so as to be helpful to the members of the performance team obviously is important. It is also useful if that plan allows you to abbreviate or elaborate your comments more or less "on the fly" depending on the dictates of available time. The simple organizational plan for an overall response commentary that is outlined in this guidebook has proven its workability. It can help you meet the organizational challenges you face in an effective fashion.

As you might imagine, the audience for your commentary, who are principally the members of the performance team, deserve your special attention. The performance team is usually poised to hear you, but it may be with mixed emotions. While on the one hand individuals may crave the kind of enlightened feedback you are prepared to deliver, they may also be somewhat apprehensive about being "judged." Most people are. Your immediate task, then, is to create an atmosphere which defuses their anxiety.

Start by greeting the members of the performance team in a relaxed and affable way. Help them to see you as an ally rather than an adversary—a fellow theatre worker who cares about the same things they do. It is appropriate that they see you in this light rather than as an Olympian figure come down to pronounce judgment on them. It helps create an atmosphere that can facilitate effective communication.

YOUR FEEDBACK

It's also a good idea to alert people, in a sentence or two, to the deliberate pattern of your response—its basic approach. This prepares your audience for what they are about to hear and cues them in as to how they can best process what you have to offer. When properly prepared the company members can listen to what you say without the psychological interference of unwarranted expectations. *Inform them that your opening comments will offer relatively detailed and disciplined description which will then be followed by your evaluations and recommendations.*

In this way you let them know you are going to provide feedback of a particular kind. Specifically it will be theatrically focused feedback intended for their use as they prepare for their next undertaking—whether that is a repeat performance or an entirely new project. Since in the great majority of instances there will not be repeat performances of the production you just witnessed it is to everyone's advantage that you couch your comments in such a way as to insure their having high transferability. That is, the principles that inform your response are best if they can be seen as having application to new theatrical ventures. The performance you just witnessed thus serves as a kind of case study. You approach it in ways that illustrate principles and practices that inform effective theatre. The feedback you provide as a performance respondent focuses upon what has been accomplished, but it does so with an eye to what the members of the performance team can subsequently utilize in the future.

OTHERS' FEEDBACK

To be sure, performance teams regularly get feedback (of sorts) from people they know, friends and relatives and others, but that feedback usually is masked as abbreviated judgments. From close acquaintances the comments are typically positive and assume some form of "You and the work you did were so good," or "The show was wonderful." Though such sentiments are welcome and undoubtedly make the recipient feel happy, they are seldom focused enough to help in the future crafting of theatre skills.

Other comments, often from journalist-reviewers, are similarly terse and judgmental, although not always so filled with praise. Let the performance team members know *the feedback you provide emphasizes performance-specific data for them to consider carefully before they appropriate it for future projects.* By phrasing it this way and by making it clear that they remain the final arbiters of any practices that might be embraced you help to empower them. Developing artists don't relish summary judgments any more than does anyone else. However, most developing artists very much appreciate learning how their work was perceived and the impact it had. They also welcome suggestions as to how they might improve. Assure them you intend to provide that kind of commentary.

In the final analysis, however, theatre artists are the ones who assume responsibility for their creative practices, and it is right that they do so. Worthy feedback helps them make responsible judgments about their artistic efforts. Of course it must be acknowledged that the immediate interest, especially for novices, usually is keyed to whether or not "you (as a spectator) liked the show" and, more particularly, their contribution to it. While that impulse on their part is understandable, you should help put it in perspective. You should take steps to keep them engaged in listening to the entire performance response commentary.

If, for example, you were to voice a judgment, positive or negative, early in your response commentary, you run the risk of tainting the communication process. When distracted by judgments which sidetrack further listening, members of the performance team may find it harder to stay open to more valuable aspects of your response. Prepare them for the fact that your evaluations of the performance will be forthcoming, but they will be offered later in your commentary. *In getting underway you will share non-valuative descriptive observations in a way that will ultimately be more useful to them.* An interesting side effect of this approach is that company members still particularly anxious to learn your evaluation of the show are likely to listen very carefully to all you have to say as they search for tell-tale clues. It is also true that when you begin your commentary by sharing descriptive observations you will find ways to organize your thoughts further and perhaps modify many of them "on the fly" to render them more useful. In this way you can supplement and embellish those thoughts about the performance that you gathered so hastily before beginning your commentary.

Your preparatory greeting is also a good time to identify the key people you will be addressing. Actors can usually be spotted, but if they have changed from their costumes and makeup even that is not always easy. I'm frequently surprised at how markedly many actors seem to differ in size and age from the characters they portray.

Also identify, in addition to the actors, the director and other key primary decision makers who may be present. Also included may be the playwright, the composer, the librettist, as well as numerous designers responsible for such things as costumes, make-up, scenery, lights, sound, and props. Music directors, fight directors, and choreographers also may be in attendance. Obviously not all these specialists are part of every show and many of them, even if they contributed to the performance, may not attend your response. But by targeting specific members of the performance team you are better able to direct your comments to those people who can profit in specific ways from what you have to say. Crew members who deal with set changes, props, costume changes, and the like also deserve to be taken into account in your response and this is a good time to lay the groundwork for that contingency.

Of course, all your introductory interactions must be brief, especially if your overall response time is limited—as it can be in some situations—to as little as three minutes or thereabouts. Hopefully, however, you will often have longer, and 45 minutes to an hour is not an excessive amount of time for a detailed commentary. The amount of response time available to you obviously has a major impact on the details you can address in your commentary, but the basic principles you employ in any instance will remain the same.

If appropriate—and the specific performance conditions will make this evident to you—a brief mention in your introductory remarks about the overall theatre event may be in order. By "the overall theatre event," I especially mean the para-aesthetics of the event. It may be that such things as auditorium temperature, passing police sirens, an intrusive thunder storm, the ambiance created by the ushers, and the like became part of the group consciousness quite apart from the aesthetic dimensions of the event. A festival which features a number of back-to-back productions also creates a special atmosphere. By briefly noting the existence of such things during your casual introductory comments you can forge an even stronger bond with the people who shared those experiences with you, and you can demonstrate that although you were aware of para-aesthetic conditions they were incidents which did not unduly dominate your response to aesthetic matters.

DESCRIPTION OF WHAT YOU PERCEIVED

The first substantive information in your commentary will be, as you noted in your introduction, a description of *what you believe you witnessed.* It is wise to regard it as what you "believe you witnessed" because it cannot be that all observations by everyone are "accurate," in the sense of being regarded and accepted as true by all observers. In this instance it is important to avoid giving the impression that you regard yours as the indisputable final words or that only your observations matter, even though you regard them as useful and important. But the performance team members should know you certainly believe in what you saw and heard and what those data add up to. In reality, you have no choice but to trust your perceptions, but given the fact that errors can occur in spite of the best of intentions, it is wise to invoke the concept of pluralistic viewing.

You can readily acknowledge that other members of the audience (and members of the performance team as well) may witness things differently from the way you do. Like you, they also trust in their observations. It is important to emphasize to the members of the performance team that all your consequent detailed descriptions and evaluations grow out of *what you believe to be your accurate perceptions—whether or not others share them.* It is also worth noting briefly that any perception, whether in the theatre or not, can arguably be considered a product of the interaction between the stimuli outside the observer's mind, in this case the theatre performance, and the predispositions, tolerances, and capabilities that reside inside the observer's mind. Each of us, to extents we cannot measure, are in many ways conditioned in advance to see what we subsequently claim (and firmly believe) we actually see—with little attention paid to our silent predispositions. It is part of your responsibility as a respondent to take that psychological phenomenon into account as you pursue your own work and urge others to do so as well. (You might want to bear in mind the frequent disparity among accounts provided by eye-witnesses to a single crime.)

The three foci of non-valuative description

With your introductory sentiments having prepared the way, you now launch into the heart of your commentary which begins, as you promised, with **description**. What you describe divides naturally into three topic areas. These topic areas are not necessarily kept discrete when you present your commentary, but it is worth noting their individual traits.

THE FICTIVE WORLD   The first focus is on the basic illusion that constitutes the fictive world. These descriptive comments focus on characters (as distinct from actors), their dominant traits (insofar as you are able to deduce them), the locale the characters inhabit (as distinct from such communicative elements as the scenery, lights, costumes, and make-up which are part of the actor's world), the deeds the characters perform, the consequences they suffer, and the apparent rules as to how things operate within this imagination-driven universe. In other words your legitimate focus is on the content and qualities of the imagination-driven fictive world.

THEATRICAL MEANS   The second focus is on the theatrical means—the materials, behaviors and techniques—that served to make the fictive world evident to you. Here you take into full account such things as acting, costumes, costume and scenic design, lighting, and all the other expressive tools utilized by the theatre collaborators. You also can describe expressive patterns within (and among) the various theatrical means. Most importantly, you pointedly link the use of these theatrical materials and techniques to the particular illusion (the kind discussed in the first topic area) they helped create. In other words you focus on the fabricated performance text.

YOUR REACTIONS TO THE FICTIVE WORLD   The focus in on your reactions—those things you found yourself thinking and feeling—*relative to the fictive world as it unfolded before you*. The reactions that are relevant within this topic area are linked directly to the fictive world. Here again the focus is not on the real actors, or scenery, or (especially) on any judgments you have about how well the theatrical performance was executed. In other words, it is simply a description of your inner life as you responded to the imagined world—the fictive world—depicted in the performance.

Descriptions are rigorously non-valuative. The most important characteristic all these topic areas share is that they are as non-valuative (insofar as
they apply to *real world* people, materials, and events) as you can make them.
In other words, these responses simply provide unadorned statements of:

1. what you believed transpired in the projected fictive world,

2. the theatrical devices and practices that were employed to
   project that image of the fictive world, and

3. your own empathetic reactions to the imagination-driven fictive
   world occurrences you witnessed.

None of the description-driven topic areas contain overt evaluations as
to whether you liked or didn't like the interpretation of the script; whether
something was or was not theatrically effective in your eyes; or whether
some aesthetic goal you believe ought to have been pursued was attained
or ignored. All those evaluative comments will come in a later section of
your commentary, after you and the members of the production company
are clear on what it was you believe you witnessed and experienced.

Your personal background may make non-valuative description difficult for you. Bear in mind that the principles that guide the descriptive
topic areas that will animate your commentary are easy to articulate here,
but not so easy to keep in mind and apply when you are actively engaged
in formulating or delivering a response. There are many reasons for this,
reasons you should methodically consider since they probably have shaped
the approaches to theatre both you and other audience members gravitate
to somewhat naturally. The personal work you do on yourself in preparing
to undertake a performance response is thus extremely important.

At the top of the list to re-examine are the habits associated with our
formal education, plus our human desire to speak authoritatively on issues,
that often get in our way as respondents. They can inadvertently militate
against following the measured procedures of a good theatrical response,
one that is geared to help a developing theatre artist understand the practical workings of theatre's fragile magic. During our student years we are
frequently enjoined to report "*what* a play means." As important as that issue
is, and it is very important, it does not do much to focus our attention on
the internal workings of theatre. Less academic attention by far is devoted
to "*how* a play (or a live performance) makes meaning" or in characterizing "what the nature of the special kind of meaning-making" in theatre
is. In part because of this shortfall in our general aesthetic education we

often find our vocabularies deficient when it comes to discussing the inner workings of theatre. Instead we resort to simplistic judgmental summaries when we discuss performances, e.g. "I liked it/I didn't like it" (a variant being "It was good/It was bad"). *As a theatre respondent you are enjoined to minimize this mode of theatre discourse with its stress on instant judgments having little support beyond your implied pronouncement of your "good taste."* It is disquieting and not very instructive. When, on the other hand, you share your shifting moment-by-moment response, even your confusion, to a performance's unfolding nature and testify to the shaping effect its elements had on your thoughts and feelings you honor one important aspect of "how" theatre generates experience and—ultimately—meaning. You draw important and much needed attention to the temporal nature of performance. You also bear witness to theatre's interpretive fecundity and to its prompting of audience reaction.

Bear in mind that performances of the same script by two or more companies will inevitably elicit different descriptions of the fictive worlds they created. Those reported performance-based fictive worlds simply differ from one another insofar as the experiences of the observers of the performance are concerned. Among other things, this phenomenon illustrates vividly the difference between the act of theatre—an evanescent time and space occurrence crafted by a team of collaborators—and what is traditionally viewed as the more stable literary artifact—the written text (or script) of the play. It also illustrates the power and place of interpretation in theatrical performance. Even with the same script serving as a starting point, each performance inevitably differs from its siblings. As you pursue your work as a performance respondent you will recognize that each version deserves a fictive world description that identifies its unique traits and honors the work of its particular performance team.

To complicate things a bit further, remember that each person viewing the same performance is likely to see it differently and thus describe and evaluate it in somewhat different terms. The nuances of their differing perceptions can be slight but they are nonetheless real and can have real impact. In some instances the differences may be so large and conspicuous that they seem at first glance to have been derived from entirely different productions. Of course this variance, slight or large, underscores why it is desirable that you, as the respondent for this performance, take time at the outset to lay out non-valuatively the specific perception base from which all your consequent comments derive. Not only does this serve as validation for the evaluations you make, it alerts the members of the performance team to the limits of your observational powers.

Let's look at the three topic areas which drive your description in a bit more illustrative detail. It is a misperception to think that your description of the fictive world can be satisfied by a bland echoing of the play's story such as might be readily abstracted from the script. A detailed retelling that closely parallels the written script (*as distinct from the performance that is based in some way on the script*) is neither the most efficient nor the most efficacious way to proceed. In the first place, it is impractical given the circumscribed time constraints within which the typical performance response proceeds. But more importantly, such a description does not effectively prepare the performance team for your comments which are predominantly **performance-specific** rather than **script-specific**. As you consider the performance text a number of fundamental issues may well emerge. For example, do the incidents depicted proceed in a causal and chronological sequence, which is very often the case, or are they fundamentally linked to each other by tonal or ideological similarities, or some combination of both? Can locales and time frames change without regard for "real world" verisimilitude? If so, is there some other organizing principle at work, such as, to name but a few, memory, triggered hallucinations, or dreams? Do animals and humans, and perhaps even inanimate objects, communicate with each other? Do the spirits of dead people co-exist with living creatures? In other words, what kind of world, in metaphysical terms, did you witness in the performance?

It is often useful to describe a performance's overall arc of action. A majority of plays (and performances) are built around a major character, the protagonist, whose fortunes rise or fall because of what they do and the obstacles they face. Your brief fictive world description can often profitably focus on that feature, the through line of occurrences which serves as a performance armature. You can prompt yourself to formulate such a description by saying "I witnessed a world in which [*here you name or otherwise characterize the protagonist*] undertook to [*here you identify the character's apparent goal*] and had to contend with [*here you list and perhaps characterize the chief obstacles*], until s/he finally [*here you articulate the character's insight or fate*]." Such an abbreviated statement is far from a complete fictive world description, but it sets the tone that enables others to understand the essential perception of the arc of action you derived from the performance. Moreover, it avoids the tedious and not very useful retelling of the play's scripted "story."

Since different performances of the same script prompt differing descriptions, depending on the emphases that emerge from particular interpretations, you should remain sensitive to the way the *particular* performance you witnessed directed your attention. This is especially true if the script is one of your favorites or one that is frequently staged. For example, in characterizing the key things you found yourself thinking and feeling during one performance you might say, "I witnessed a world in which a despondent young man sought to overcome his sense of abandonment and psychological desolation by sorting through supernatural and other messages until he finally exacted revenge for the wrongs done him and his family."

For another performance you might say, "I witnessed a world in which a clever young man feigned madness until he could maneuver his enemies into a vulnerable position and in so doing he over-reached and lost his own life."

In viewing still another you might say, "I witnessed a young son who had difficulties making up his mind as to how and when he might exact the revenge for his father's death until he finally acquiesced to the words of his father's spirit and in doing so went to a psychologically peaceful but physically violent death."

Yet another performance might prompt you to say, "I witnessed a world wherein a prince had to confront a decadent and corrupt society and though he strove to set things aright he could only punish the principal villains and had to leave it to others to straighten out the affairs of the country."

Of course, these examples sample just a small range of possible performances (and interpretations) that might appear under the name *Hamlet*. There could be many, many more each based on ostensibly the same scripted story, but each with its own *performance emphases and underlying intentions.* Each performance sets forth its own fictive world and apparent arc of action. Each perforce differs, by a lot or a little, from the imagined world circumstances and arcs that are central to other performances. As a respondent you undertake to describe the fictive world that characterizes *one performance as you witnessed it,* without voicing (at this point) corrective admonitions or preferential judgments. In essence it is appropriate to assume and proceed as if each performance team set forth precisely the image of the fictive world it intended to set forth. Your job, at this juncture, is merely to bear honest and detailed witness to their efforts and to that world.

Not all brief fictive world descriptions are best characterized by tracing the protagonist's arc of motivation and fortunes. It all depends on the ways the performance "programs" your responses. Alternatively you can choose, for example, to describe the nature of the world the characters inhabit in terms of the tensions and tone it manifests. Such a comment might be "The fictive world I witnessed was rife with decadence and social decay which oppressed the characters but motivated one of them to challenge the power of the corrupt leaders in charge." Or you might see a fictive world "in which the bulk of the characters exhibited a great deal of personal enjoyment even when the main character hesitated to take advantage of the opportunity to bond with his/her true love due to a trivial miscommunication." Or perhaps what you witnessed showed that the spark for each incident "was a deep-seated need for revenge (or pleasure) on the part of all the major characters." It may be that "the sense of inevitability that pervaded the world served to neutralize every character's attempts to bring about much-needed change or improvement."

The point to be made is that your brief description of the fictive world as you perceived it, however phrased, opens the way for a fuller consideration of what the performance team sparked in your mind. The brief fictive world description which you strive to articulate for yourself before you begin the actual public commentary is very important. It calls upon you to be sensitive to your inner sense of the performance and to be honest and unguarded with yourself. It will serve as the basic framework on which you hang your further observations. The more detail you ultimately provide, the clearer will be the team's sense of the impact their work had on you. Added description beyond your initial comments makes even clearer the nature of the theatrical image that you perceived replete with the contexts (physical, psychological, etc.) within which the characters strove to accomplish their goals. All this is necessary if the performance team is to assess how successful their efforts were—at least in affecting you. And therein lies an important leitmotif inherent in all that the respondent does and says.

Importantly, the respondent provides data and perspective that enable the performance team members to assess their work themselves. In the final analysis you, as a respondent, seek to empower these developing artists so that they can function fully and effectively on their own. It is clearly important for you to begin your formal response with a brief statement that characterizes the dominant traits of the overall fictive world. That statement frames the basic discussion and gets you underway. But it is equally important for you to take pains to amplify your fictive world characterization at subsequent points in your extended commentary. Your later descriptions of the basic workings of the fictive world intermingle with your descriptions of the theatrical means you were made aware of as well as your moment-by-moment response to the occurrences onstage. Presented as non-valuative and interlocking descriptions, they exemplify the richness of your perceptions and of the fictive world stimuli that prompted them. The members of the performance team are free to draw upon your words in order to measure their own sense of accomplishment.

There are some ego-based respondent pitfalls. While serving as a respondent you may find yourself subtly motivated to "get it right" or to ally yourself with the supposed intentions of the performance team. However, you do not serve them well by allowing your comments to be shaped by personal, largely self-serving, impulses. What the team members most need from you is an honest and detailed response, as full as the available time and your capabilities will allow, so that they can appraise on their own what a trained theatre observer actually witnessed and by implication the relative success of their work. There is no "right" perception on your part beyond the one that is faithful to what you observed taking place. Another way of saying this is that you must put all your ego-driven motivations aside and allow your trained skills and insights to be offered in such a way as to serve the needs of the developing theatre artists you address. On a related note, you do well to resist the impulse to display your own literacy by referring to canonical works you regard as having something in common with the performance you just witnessed. Similarly, avoid referring to your own production successes (or failures.) In short, attempting to enhance your personal credentials by any means apart from a concentrated focus on the work at hand is likely to backfire. Performance team members desire, and have every right to expect, that it is *their* work which is being honestly anatomized and appraised. The best measure of that, in their eyes (and mine), is the intensity, sensitivity, and precise focus of your responsive commentary.

Describe the theatrical means affecting you. Your overall description of the fictive world aligns you with the inner life of the imagined alternate reality. You naturally extend your reach and refine your commentary as you add *your descriptions of the theatrical means and your empathic response to the fictive world*. The intertwined descriptions focus on and array three kinds of data simultaneously, data you methodically link together: you amplify and offer detailed examples of your "fictive world" perceptions. You target specific practices embedded in the "real world" performance text. Finally, you identify the thoughts and feelings that were generated by your empathic connection to the fictive world.

Consider multiple "theatre languages." In considering the theatrical means employed in the performance text it is useful to regard them as diverse communicative techniques that comprise the many "languages" of the theatrical performance. Each element in the performance text derives its eloquence from the illusion it helps create and from its potency within the synergistic whole of the overall performance. *Your bifurcated response describes the linkage between the perceived inner life of the fictive world and the specific real world practices employed by the theatre workers to fuel those perceptions.* In other words, in offering this part of your commentary you direct your attention to actors as well as characters, to scenery as well as fictive locales, to costumes as well as character attire, and so forth. In this way your specific theatre expertise boldly comes to the fore.

Of course, your analysis of the linkage between the performance text and the illusion it created extends even further each developing theatre artist's capacity for self-assessment. If, as they listen to you, they see your perceptions match their intentions, they can judge their contributions to be successful—at least with you. If your perceptions and their intentions seem not to be in harmony, the members of the performance team can see that something has gone awry. It may be that their work on crafting and executing the various aspects of the performance text was sub-par. They can be guided to a clear appraisal of their work. But it may also be that your ability to respond to the performance text may seem to be at fault. If a communication shortfall proves to be the case, it is important for both you and the performance team to recognize both contingencies. In reality, a single and simple root cause for any performance/perception misfire is difficult to identify with simple and absolute certainty. However, by continuing to provide detailed descriptions of the performance text and the potency of its constituent parts as you experienced them, you increase the likelihood of isolating the source for any dissonance. In large part this is a consequence of your operating as an ally of the performance team who join you in the quest for the well-springs of theatre's fragile magic.

We can readily agree that every performance text is multi-faceted. It is also designed to be witnessed (or "read") by its spectators as it unfolds in time and space. Its means (or "languages") are the various specialized cueing systems the creative collaborators have used to form the performance text. We easily can see, as you know from your own artistry, that in actual practice the performance text emerges as a very complex stimulus. Most importantly, perhaps, a great many of its constituent elements are transitory. They exist, and then very rapidly cease to exist, in real time and real space. They appear and almost immediately disappear in the presence of the spectator who witnesses them as they pass by at enactment speed.

Gestures, an inflection, a simulated discovery, a change in lighting are all very quickly relegated to a spectator's memory and imagination. But while they exist at the moment of the spectator's perception, they can be said to unlock the power of theatrical performance.

The illusion of immediacy is at the heart of most (some might say all) theatrical presentation. Playwrights, directors, and actors labor long and hard to make it appear to audiences that what is occurring on stage is happening for the first time. The late nineteenth and early twentieth century American actor William Gillette wrote meaningfully about the phenomenon in *The Illusion of the First Time in Acting*. American playwright Thornton Wilder refers to this unique characteristic of theatre as the "perpetual present." Other writers and theorists invoke this same basic sense of immediacy when they talk about a play's "action" or "doing" or "becoming." The unique thrill that audiences experience when they see something *enacted* (as distinct from something being talked about, indicated, or alluded to) derives in large measure from this defining trait of theatre performance. Although it is mercurial and elusive, a perceived **present action** is clearly the source of much of theatre's power. But what must be stressed is that the illusion of immediacy or spontaneity in theatre is just that, an **illusion**. Because it is an illusion, and a highly crafted one at that, it deserves to be examined to determine just what goes into making it work.

Theatre languages exist in the real world. Importantly, all the theatre languages (cues) in a performance text, whether fleeting or a bit more persistent, are publicly accessible. They can readily be perceived by the spectators. In fact, they are designed to be perceived. Included are, among other things, costumes, lighting and scenic displays, the verbal and non-verbal behavior of the actors, their make-up, the choreographed shaping of their behavior by directors (including the specialized activities of dancing and fighting) and, when applicable, singing. In other words, all the performance-based stimuli that strike the eye and ear (and thus stimulate the imagination) of the spectator are appropriately thought of as theatre languages. The particular ways they are employed—that is, the way they are selected, shaped, combined and modulated—enable each audience member who perceives them to envision a fictive world that is wholly imagined. Ideally each spectator's envisioning provides a replica which matches the imagination-based fictive world that guided the theatre workers as they created the performance text in the first place. At least that is what happens when things go according to plan.

It is worth emphasizing that the only way any spectator (including you as respondent) recognizes what is going on in the imagination-based fictive world is because each of you interprets (and allows yourself to be affected by) the theatre languages that animate the performance text in the real world. Nowhere is this more important than when you are surveying and assessing a character's inner life. Characters, like people in real life, reveal their dominant dispositions (friendly, cantankerous, forgiving, etc,) by their actions. Similarly their motivations, deliberations, and decisions are understood on the basis of what the spectator sees and hears them do. No one really "knows" the inner life of another human being or character (no matter how sure they may be that they do) except as they deduce it (or, in effect, imagine it) from observing that person or character carefully. The fact that you may feel you know and understand the dispositions, thoughts, feelings, and motivations that you believe a character is experiencing is testimony to the actor's expertise and to the focus of your capacity for empathy. They both figure prominently in the fostering of theatre's fragile magic.

It is also worth noting that the theatre languages used in the performance text, though publicly accessible, are subject to distortion (and dissonance) if inexpertly employed by the members of the performance team or inadequately read by any spectator. But though an error-induced shortfall may turn out to be the source of any dissonance you can eventually identify, it makes good sense while witnessing the performance to continue to assume that every performance team member is suitably insightful and expressively capable and made intentional decisions. Otherwise, your premature judgments, whether positive or negative, ill-conceived or accurate, can skew your ability to freely experience or describe the remainder of the performance. You should avoid such a derailing pitfall. There will be ample time for you to evaluate the proceedings in a balanced fashion when all the data are witnessed and have excited your imagination. When that step in the overall process has been reached you are both ready and well equipped to describe to the members of the production company your response to the performance in as much detail as can be mustered.

You undertake an especially important task when you set about to actively connect the image of the fictive world you harbor within you to the relevant theatre languages embedded in the real world performance text. You will undoubtedly spend a good deal of intellectual energy identifying and linking them. You will find that it is not always easy to allow these twin objects of your attention, the theatrical stimulus and your spectatorial response, to travel parallel routes in your awareness. For example, if you witness a character you reckon to be uninhibited and flamboyant you will charged to identify the cues that prompted your perception. As you confront this situation you almost certainly will be able to target multiple cues provided by several discrete theatre language systems. Let's look at a primitive (and overstated) example just to illustrate some things about the process.

Turn over in your mind the following sample thoughts. Did you note that, in projecting the image of an uninhibited and flamboyant character, the actor employed rapid speech patterns and buoyant movement (acting behavior), wore brightly colored, stylish or even risqué garb (costume design)? Was it make-up that allowed you to see a character as old (make-up design)? Did a follow spot highlight the actor's entrance and on-stage movements (lighting design)? Did other characters move away or register dismay when the character in question appeared on the scene (ensemble acting and directorial blocking), or, alternatively, did they cluster around the character in an apparent bid for attention (also ensemble acting and directorial blocking)? In short, what theatre cues in the performance text, these or others, enabled you to imaginatively perceive the fictive character in the specific way you did? Which ones seemed to carry the most freight? Did all of them operate in harmony or were some either missing or countervailing?

In other words, this topic in your commentary deals with all the publicly accessible cueing systems that go together to create the performance text. That performance text, in turn, bodies forth the image of the fictional world in real time and space. As you witnessed the performance text, visual and aural cues triggered your perceptions, your imagination, your thoughts, and your feelings. A psychological image of the performance became part of your experiential consciousness. Your tracing out of that process provides important data for the performance team's consideration.

Notice that although these performance text languages may have initially been motivated by (and can often be confirmed by) the relatively persistent words of the script, *they belong most of all to the transient realm of time/space-based performance*. It is not that the words from the script which are uttered by the actors are unimportant; it is simply that your specialized efforts as a theatre respondent encourage you to focus heavily on the elusive extra-verbal nature of performance. All the dialogue the playwright has written reaches you through the filtering and enabling presence of the performers. The script as it is realized in performance is ultimately that particular incarnation of the script that draws your professional focus.

In all your efforts you work on behalf of the developing theatre artists to illumine and clarify for them the fragile, and elusive, magic of theatre performance. Performance texts (theatre performances) are—in their essential natures—remarkably, sometimes frustratingly, evanescent. These qualities shape and influence much of your on-going efforts.

There are some daunting practical challenges you will encounter in meeting the demands of this topic area within your oral commentary.

First of all, as you undoubtedly realize, there is an almost infinite number of stimuli in the performance text that can affect you. To attempt to refer to them all would make your response commentary very long—much longer than the actual performance.

In the second place many of the influential performance text elements can be adjudged by your auditors to be so obvious that merely naming them can become tedious and make it appear that you are gilding the lily. Should this happen, your listeners may well simply tune out.

A third closely related issue arises in planning the efficient use of your time. You want to be able to complete the full arc of your response—including evaluation and recommendations—and you cannot afford to get bogged down in this data-intensive section of your feedback response. Obviously, for all these reasons, you must choose judiciously what to actually include in this part of your commentary. Your taste, intelligence, and theatre savvy are your best allies, but there are some general guidelines you should consider as you proceed.

Keep in mind that every honest description you offer of any fictive world element has the virtue of increasing the performance team members' awareness of what you witnessed. As we have already noted, their eventual understanding of your perceptions enables them to evaluate their theatrical impact; if, in the final analysis, you can assist them to do that you have nurtured a valuable kind of empowerment, one sorely needed by developing theatre artists. Your identification of specific contributions (in acting, costume design, lighting, etc.) highlights each individual's role in forging the performance text. To be sure, you are likely to focus on those aspects of the fictive world which most stimulated your imagination, but on the other side of the coin you should also take into account subtler contributions as well. Its collaborative nature dictates that theatre must draw upon the diverse efforts of numerous specialists, not all of whom make flashy contributions. It is important for all who hear your response to recognize the ways their less obvious efforts serve to support the work of their colleagues. This is a fundamental insight worth promoting in the minds of developing theatre artists.

As we have noted, the third topic area animating your commentary details your intellectual and emotional involvement in the fictive world. Some attention has already been paid to this issue, but more clarification can prove helpful. When addressing this concern you offer your amplified reactions to the *fictive lives the characters were living*. For example, did you feel the character you identify as the protagonist was strongly or weakly motivated in pursuit of a credible goal? Was each character's goal clear or were you hesitant to trust their stated objective? And as you imaginatively entered into the fictive world did the struggles encountered there suggest parallels to issues you identify in the world you live in outside the theatre (for example racial tensions, overweening self interest, or naïve gullibility)? Did you vicariously suffer or rejoice with any of the characters? Were their inner lives accessible to you? Did you change your opinions during the course of the performance about any matters in the fictive world? Did anything in the fictive world prompt you to change your thinking about any real world analogs? In short, how did you respond in your heart and mind to the tensions and pressures contained in the alternate reality you witnessed?

Keep in mind, however, that your judgments apply to characters and situations within the fictive world and the referents they suggest in the real world. As such they are important reactions to (and aspects of) your fictive world description, but *they are not judgments about the relative expertise of the performance team*. They are extensions of the performance text and its impact. They remain, in a special sense of the word, non-valuative. They describe the impact of the performance text on one willing and capable observer—you. But they are not sufficient as performance evaluations.

Therefore it is formally appropriate for you to say that Hamlet was neurotic and mentally troubled but inappropriate to say, *at this point*, that the actor playing Hamlet was nervous, insecure, and unsure of himself. The former addresses life in the fictive world, the latter appraises behavior in the real world. Similarly, it is appropriate to note that Ophelia dressed more like a peasant or a slut than like a member of the court, but inappropriate to say that the costume designer has no taste. While you may be strongly tempted at this point to offer your summary of the production's final (eventual) "meaning," or your judgment of the performance's quality or worth, it is important for you to resist that temptation. Those pronouncements will come a bit later. Instead, you here chronicle the nature of the shifting awareness you experienced during the production's enactment time. In this way you pay tribute to the fundamental temporal nature of the performance, the way the "ever present now" unfolds and transmutes during the course of the performance.

EMPOWERING DEVELOPING THEATRE ARTISTS TO BE SELF-ACTUATING

What you have done by means of your non-valuative description of: (1) the fictive world, (2) the performance text, and (3) your response to them is to provide the performance team members with the data they can use to survey and evaluate their own work. By your staying within the bounds outlined here, the performance team members can observe you have allowed your insights and skills as a qualified theatre worker and observer to serve their needs as developing theatre artists. You have extended their artistic awareness. They are free to judge their accomplishments and their shortfalls in a non-defensive manner and in the privacy of their own minds and studios. While it yet remains for you to place their work in a larger evaluative context, the descriptions provided in your commentary thus far can help them achieve a healthy self-awareness. It may well be that this is the most valuable service of your commentary as a whole.

6

EVALUATIONS AND RECOMMENDATIONS

Once you've delivered the descriptive portion of your commentary it is time for you to share your frank evaluative comments and recommendations with the performance team. In doing so you focus on, and offer judgments, as to how well they formulated, crafted, and executed their creative decisions. Because you have already described in some detail what you witnessed in the performance your auditors should have a clear understanding of your evaluative targets. It is worth remembering that the earlier detailed and non-valuative descriptions you voiced provided crucial data for the members of the performance team's self-actualized efforts to develop artistic awareness and development. In short, those data facilitated the judging of their work that the team members do themselves, much of which happens privately after your commentary is concluded. Your judgments and recommendations at this point in your commentary are valuable because they reflect outside perspectives and tastes. Keep in mind that a central objective of your work as a respondent is to aid the developing theatre artists (whose work you have witnessed) to grow and mature. They can do that both by comparing their intentions with their accomplishments (as in the act of self appraisal) and by seeing their work in the context of larger perspectives (which you now provide).

THE EVALUATIVE CHALLENGE

As a practicing respondent you continue to face a number of challenges and cautions. For example, when you offer your appraisals it is important to link your judgments to the criteria against which you measure the performance team's work. As has already been emphasized, it does not contribute much to developing artists' growth for them to hear only simplistic personal appraisals such as "I liked it" or "I didn't like it" or "It was good" or "It was not good." Developing theatre artists profit most from understanding the bases and principles upon which particular judgments rest. From the performance team's perspective the underlying precepts you invoke provide principled support for your evaluations as well as standards they might choose to live by. The team members trust you to be a knowledgeable, discerning and responsive spectator, and they have good cause to do so. You have spent personal and professional time forging an understanding of theatre performance from a producing artist's point of view. Now you unflinchingly focus on the nature and details of the single live theatre performance they have put forth. In providing your detailed and thoughtful response you are doing what other audience members have likely done only in a passing fashion and with scattered results.

Whether or not your assessments and standards ultimately turn out to be comfortably aligned with those held by the performance team, it is nonetheless important for you to articulate them. That enables the developing artists whom you seek to serve to see even more clearly where you are coming from. It also allows them to expand their aesthetic goals. But it will not always be easy for you to articulate in a precise and clear fashion the bases on which you make your aesthetic judgments, at least at first. It is more likely that the underlying premises that shape your reactions will appear to be elusive, more in the realm of inexplicable "feelings" than communicable principles arising from a disciplined and rational base. They may seem to hover just out of reach of your consciousness and you may think them to be inaccessibly instinctual or sub-conscious. But if you trust your spectator-based responses and methodically subject them to thoughtful, self-reflective analysis the chances are very good that you will finally discern what underlying criteria, whether previously articulated or not, were at work to shape your relative embrace of the performance. In a practical sense this exercise promotes one of the most valuable personal growth benefits you will experience whenever you serve as a respondent. You will grow to trust even more what may be described as your largely intuitional aesthetic sensibility, that *je ne sais quoi* that so often is linked to artistic talent, while at the same time you subject it to the healthy analytic power of your rational mind.

Described yet another way, as a respondent you have opened yourself to the informing power of the performance by setting aside—to the fullest extent you could—biases, expectations, and personal preferences. You have disciplined yourself to be an ideal spectator. You have functioned as a willing and obliging observer and allowed the performance itself to determine the parameters of your empathic experience. That performance, by impressing itself on your responsive nature, made the style and content of its fictive world a part of your experiential awareness. In order to formulate your evaluations and suggestions for the developing artists' future growth you are now free to probe your reactions and appraise the performance's impact on you, both in positive and negative terms, as a measure of its aesthetic success. In short, you now "read" the performance's relative excellence by scanning the recent history and potency of your own informed and disciplined experiential response.

As you know from your own experience—and as we have noted in earlier chapters—the array of theatre productions you are likely to encounter as a respondent constitutes a very diverse universe. Aesthetic styles, production intentions, and the internal rationales of differing fictive worlds vary widely. This can easily mean that a particular performance practice aesthetically appropriate to one production could be anathema to another. It also means that a judgment based on a standard appropriate to one production can easily miss the mark if applied to a very different—but nonetheless defensible—production. In other words, you cannot simply apply pre-digested standards or maintain personal staging preferences for each work you witness. The varied works you will likely witness call for individualized responses and judgments. This puts a special pressure on you to remain flexible and broadly aware of diverse aesthetic approaches and options. It also means you must stay as responsive as you can to the widest range of theatrical expression. But, though you remain open-minded and capable of viewing a wide range of theatre work, you can also take solace in knowing that it is a central obligation of the performance team, through the medium of their work, to guide you to the aesthetic criteria applicable to the specific performance. The performance itself assists you to respond to the power (the sought-after magic) of theatre practice.

Inevitably your evaluations will be conditioned by your own aesthetic preferences and experiences. It could not be otherwise. But it is also true that you are a knowledgeable professional in the field. You are also able to identify and even champion the likely judgments of others whom you represent as a kind of surrogate spokesperson. In short, while, in the first instance, you recognize what kind of theatre "works" for you, it is also true that you have a strong sense of what kind of theatre probably "works" or can "work" for others. Stated in other terms, your evaluations and recommendations focus on that fragile and magical state wherein a theatrical performance "works" for you and, to the extent you can imagine it, for others.

Although at least some of your evaluations and suggestions will differ from those advanced by other auditors it remains highly likely that the bulk of them will, at the very least, touch upon broad issues of theatre artistry that loom as important to all knowledgeable spectators. Admittedly, any alternate staging possibilities you outline as part of your commentary may not turn out to be preferred choices in the minds of the performance team, but when you offer them as practical examples they clarify further the character of your perceptions and allow the team members to continue to appraise the way you framed their work in your mind.

It would be a mistake for you to regard your respondent-specific offerings as impotent when they do not supersede the performance teams' choices. Their principal value ultimately lies in the ways they stimulate, clarify and stabilize the creative thinking of the performance team. In confronting your assessments and the bases on which they rest, the performance team is put in a good position to review in even more detail their own assumptions, an enterprise that will inevitably make them more reflective and responsible theatre artists.

Bear in mind that it is not your goal as a respondent to determine or forge congruency of all spectators' tastes. Rather it is your task to target performance-specific practices that are most likely to command an audience's attention and influence its perceptions. Any adverse judgments you make will focus on performance behaviors which, subjectively speaking, interrupted the performance's effectiveness for you and, arguably, for other spectators as well. On the other hand your endorsing judgments will ratify ways in which the performance was successful—at least for you. Any consequent recommendations you advance merely suggest things the performance team might profitably consider should they wish to modify their practice in future undertakings.

It is important to recognize that, in spite of all your suggestions and recommendations, you are not charged with dictating fail-safe theatre practice. Not only is that an end unlikely to ever be realized, the mere invocation of it is counter productive to your aims and probably to those of the performance team as well. Psychologically speaking, it is the ongoing search for that personally resonant and "elusive something that works" that keeps most developing theatre artists (and you) actively involved in creating theatre performances. In a word, it is what keeps them (and you) "developing." If you think about it, you can easily recognize from your own practical theatre experience that "what works" changes as exigent circumstances, and your experiences/tastes, change. It is a significant dimension of theatre's fragile magic.

Finally, for humility's sake, if nothing else, it is also worth reminding yourself that as a respondent who views the performance from the "outside" you labor under some unavoidable limitations. For example, you can't know with certainty the working conditions that informed the specific choices the team made (or felt forced to make) in bringing the performance to life at this time and in this place. Perhaps some of your practical suggestions will echo practices the team already experimented with before finally scrapping them as undertakings that "did not work." However, by simply voicing them, along with any others you may think of, you bring again to the "table of the creative mind" an array of alternative performance strategies.

TAPPING INTO AND STIMULATING THE CREATIVE PROCESS

It is almost certainly true that herein lies one of your worthiest contributions in offering performance recommendations. You have the opportunity to re-stimulate the team's formulary thinking so they can consider afresh the creative processes that determined their evident performance choices. From that revivified vantage point they are more likely to explore and evaluate possible alternatives anew even as they come to understand more fully the relative potency of the choices they have already made. In a practical sense, your recommendations need not rectify all performance shortfalls (however nice that might seem) in order to be worthy. They simply have to set forth credible possibilities that the members of the team can reflect on while considering again how their performance—or any future variant of it—might be re-crafted so as to effectively generate an even richer experience and resonant meaning for theatre audiences. Your recommendations help them re-imagine the parameters and the species of decision-making that characterized their earliest creative thinking. You help them to reengage with their creative processes. You help them to imagine themselves being "back at the drawing board."

It should be evident that as a theatre respondent you function as a specialized breed of teacher. By means of your commentary you are in position to promote a broad and practical awareness of the multi-pronged and complex way theatrical productions really come into being. Your task is to direct critical attention to the work of many people who have contributed to the final product—the performance. As you well know from your own production experience there are many people who, though seldom if ever seen, nonetheless contribute to the performance in ways which bear on its relative success.

Let me repeat an example I have cited earlier. Relatively anonymous and invisible members of the performance team (as broadly conceived) often have a major influence on significant aspects of the theatre event's **para-aesthetic nature**. Some of those para-aesthetic workers promote (publicize) the show to the public. Posters, ad campaigns, programs, and media interviews are among their pre-event undertakings. As a respondent you draw attention to the de facto practice of theatre when you assess even briefly the effectiveness of their efforts. In your role as a teacher/respondent you help direct focus on many workers whose contributions are often either overlooked or simply taken for granted. If you use your immediate response to your performance experience as a measure when appraising pre-performance promotion, you can consider, evaluate and offer suggestions dealing with such issues as: "Does their work prepare audiences for an appropriate encounter with the performance *per se*? Are there ways that the audience experience might be enhanced? Are the expectations the pre-show materials generated appropriate ones? Did they cue you into dimensions of the performance which extended your performance experience?" This becomes a useful way to provide feedback to those who work on promotion while at the same time educating all members of the performance team about the important work of one of the most ignored sub-groups.

EVALUATE PARA-AESTHETIC CONCERNS AS FACTORS

Of course, there are many other para-aesthetic factors that also can have a noteworthy impact on the members of the audience. Broadly speaking, the para-aesthetic features of the theatre event are best judged by their influence on audience members' safety and comfort. Here your judgments (and any alternative suggestions that grow out of those judgments) include such things as: "What is the extent to which you feel welcomed into the audience space? How effective was the ambient music, lighting, and usher behavior in creating a secure and safe psychological and physical environment for you?" Of course, it occasionally is true that deviations from psychological safety and security are deliberately employed. Particular performances can thrive on a para-aesthetic mood of threat and anxiety. (For example, having uniformed "Nazis" serving as ushers for productions of *Cabaret* is a practice that has been used on several occasions.) It is up to you to be alert to such contingencies and adjudge them accordingly. The test of their potency is, in effect, how you appraise the effectiveness of their impact on you. The awareness you are promoting is that para-aesthetic issues are part of what a performance team must address.

Keep a healthy balance between the two components of the theatre event. Do not lose sight of the fact that however influential para-aesthetic issues are, the core of the theatre performance is its aesthetic component. Your empathic connection to that component is though the performance text. In effect, the performance text serves as the sensory emblem of a production's fictive world. On one hand it exists and functions in the real world. It is constituted of corporeal materials. However, on the other hand its inner nature is determined by the pressures and tensions of the fictive world that it bodies forth in analog fashion. It thus provides the audience with an accessible (sensory) portal to the performance team's imagination-based creation. When they attend closely to the performance text audiences come to understand the complex imaginative workings of the fictive world. Of course for this to take place the performance text must be fully perceptible. It must be seen and heard. (There are also a limited number of instances in which other senses such as smell and touch may be utilized.) It provides a sensory experience. Therefore, as a respondent you evaluate, at its basic level, how well the performance text could be perceived. If, for example, the actors could not be seen or heard clearly, the effectiveness of the performance text must be considered compromised. If the lighting was so dim that you could not identify characters and what they were doing the basic sensory communication was put in jeopardy. In other words, one of your elemental tasks is to judge the performance team's effectiveness in meeting the threshold obligations whereby the performance text was appropriately seen and heard.

Thus far your judgments about both the para-aesthetic contexts and the transmission of the performance text's visual and aural signals are simple and direct. Your subsequent evaluation of the performance text is more complex. This later portion of your evaluation provides a critical assessment of those finely honed aesthetic decisions that inform the fictive world. It is at this juncture in your presentation that you are most likely to be challenged. After all, it is a relatively straightforward task for you to assert whether or not an actor was audible or a piece of stage business could be observed. The larger and more telling aesthetic import of what was witnessed, on the other hand, is more sophisticated and sometimes even problematic. When you provide this species of judgment the specter of possible partisan interpretation can again be raised. As we have noted earlier, the imagination-based experiences you witnessed and participated in vicariously along with the meanings you attribute to the performance are inevitably viewed by others as personal responses and thereby susceptible to charges of bias or error. Nonetheless, it is this portion of your commentary that—for most people—provides the most meaningful thrust of your work. More than any other part of your commentary, your assessment of the production's fictive world and its workings fuels your efforts as a respondent.

THEATRICAL PERFORMANCE OFFERS EXPERIENCE

The theatre respondent focuses on the experience generated by the performance. The fullest measure of a theatrical performance *per se*, its potency and fragile magic—the determination of how well it "works" —lies in its power to generate vivid and responsive audience experiences. To be sure, philosophies, credos, and ideas are woven through, but are not entirely synonymous with, theatrically generated performance experiences. At root, theatrically generated performance experiences derive from a spectator's empathic sense of a compelling fictive life. Ideas, credos, and philosophic arguments can be, and are, derived from a consideration of that fictive life, but it is the core fictive life that remains primary to the experience of theatrical performance. It is true that both the ideas generated by a performance (what might be called its content) and the theatrical vitality of that performance (the extent to which it engaged and maintained your attention) are important to the respondent, but the two should not be unduly conflated.

Your focus is on "theatrical" effectiveness. It is possible, for example, for a performance to set forth worthy ideas (meaning) but nonetheless be theatrically tepid. Similarly, a performance can be exciting and compelling to an audience without providing any telling reference to significant higher thoughts. These twin goals animate the best of theatre performances. As every practicing theatre artist can testify, experiential audience responsiveness is inevitably woven into the essential nature of live theatrical performance. But it is evident that audience responsiveness is not monolithic. As you know, what "works" for one group of spectators is not assured of "working" for another. This exposes any appraisals of performance to possible question and challenge. The best one can hope for is that enlightened audience responsiveness, such as yours, provides a comprehensive base that can clarify a performance's most meaningful transactions. As a respondent you frankly assess how well and in what ways the performance "worked" or, conversely, fell short of that elusive goal of excellence—insofar as you can determine it.

REMAINING OPEN-MINDED

As you surely realize by now in our discussion, you must take pains to keep your evaluation from being parochial or too tied to strictly personal preferences. Similarly, your approval or disapproval of performance effectiveness cannot rest solely on your allegiances or aversions to the ideas you feel are being espoused—to the script as a source of "content." In fact, your most important task as a theatre respondent is oriented in a slightly different direction. Although the resonance of ideas generated by the performance is noteworthy and figure in your overall evaluation, those ideas do not command your principal (and defining) attention. As a theatre respondent you are resolutely focused on *the fragility and magic of live performance*. It is the theatrical workings of the presentation that attracts the bulk of your professional focus. To be sure the ideas embedded in a performance cannot and should not be shunned. But they are considered as they are intertwined with the evocative dynamics of performance *per se*. These two mutually supportive elements generate their own synergism and must be evaluated accordingly.

THE THEATRE RESPONDENT'S SPECIAL NICHE

It is characteristic of our educational milieu that there is no paucity of teachers who will energetically direct the developing artists' attention to *what a play means, what significance it holds in adumbrating a culture, what its power is to reveal facets of the author's life story,* and—to speak in general terms—*what constitutes its ideational content.* But assisting a developing artist to recognize *how a performance (and by implication a performed play) makes meaning* is less earnestly practiced. It is this precisely this facet of the developing artist's growth that is importantly and directly addressed by you as a theatre respondent. It is your ability and determined commitment to focus intensely on the nature of theatrical performance, how it is effectively fashioned and how it imparts a special evocative power to a play's ideational content that enables you to make an especially worthy—and much needed—contribution to the developing artist's growth.

One preferred way of doing this is to loosen your commentary from the constraints of narrowly conceived or biased judgments by referencing the broad traits of performances that function at their best. In other words, you do well to nest your personal spectator-based experience and your judgments within the contexts of how theatre's elusive and fragile magic most often can be seen to "work" in the dynamic milieu of performance.

Spectator experience is a key measure of performance effectiveness. As we said earlier, spectators for whom particular performances "work" testify to their being satisfying at a profound level. They capture the audience's attention and maintain their interest throughout. In spite of the fact that the bulk of those spectators may passingly—and without providing detail—declare such performances to be well conceived, carefully crafted, and precisely executed, it is more probable that, at root, they are primarily reacting to the fullness and richness of their own inner experience and only secondarily to the identifiable traits of the performance. Importantly, it is also your inner experience as a respondent that provides you with the initial touchstone for your evaluation. But the key differences between you and the casual general spectator lie in your superior command of the many "languages" and strategies associated with theatrical performance, as well as your insistence on remaining non-valuative until all data are in.

Your experience of a performance guides your analytic evaluation. The extent to which your attention and interest are stimulated by a theatrical performance nonetheless remains a fair measure of its overall success. But your merely articulating that measure does not fulfill your responsibilities as a respondent. You also are obligated to identify the expressive devices of the performance text, their organization and the ways they coalesced to provoke your reaction. You must remember that the comparative contributions of performance-based stimuli differ from show to show. It is primarily for this reason that a simple weighted checklist assigning uniform values across the board to each theatrical "language" of a so-called "typical" performance text is unlikely to capture the fragile magic at work in any particular show. The synergism that informs each individual performance text is both fragile and unique. Your responses undertake to unlock the dynamics of those combinations and in so doing they probe the magic of the theatrical transaction. It is also true that your judgments will be more user-friendly if you identify parallels between the impact of a particular production practice and the essential nature of theatrical performance itself. This is especially true in the case of action unfolding in the ongoing "now" of theatre's perpetual present. Theatrical performances are not static. The inner life—or action of the performance—unfolds and develops. Each "now" moment of that action is replaced by a succeeding one. That one, in turn, is replaced by the next and so on and so on. The manner, tempo, and pattern of the performance's unfolding and development virtually dictate the spectator's experience.

The performance triggers your honed theatrical sense. As we've noted above, it is the performance itself which largely dictates the criteria you should use in appraising it. Typically the criteria are already in your mind and you invoke them to make your judgments. You call them out in response to the kind of performance you believe you are witnessing. For example, "Do you see the style of fictive world as realistic? Does it unfold in accordance with readily recognized causal and quotidian precepts? Is it representative of a real world time and place? Is it peopled with characters who bear important similarities to real-world personae?" To the extent these characteristics are present the performance team is asking you—in part—to appraise their accuracy in depicting a simulacrum of real world events. In other words, you offer a comparative judgment between the fictive world of the performance and the real world referents that exist outside of the performance. But you should not oversimplify your tasks or be misled. Your theatrical sense still reigns paramount and will, if necessary, trump your historical knowledge base. Thus while it is appropriate for you to scan the performance for anachronisms such as inappropriate/ appropriate garb or props or settings or relationships among characters, any apparent anomalies must be carefully appraised for their immediate theatrical expressiveness. Often theatrical power derives from intentional "anachronisms," unique ingredients in an otherwise uniform historical mix. Once again it is your sensitive theatrical awareness that enables you to make this important determination.

Performances cue in your standards. Performances that are built around precepts other than strict realism enlarge your field of investigation. Musicals, to cite a popular example, invoke their own judgmental criteria simply by dint of their performance style. Singing, dancing, hyperbolic character behaviors and accompanying music increases the performance's sensory input. But those same elements urge you to respond to more than immediate sensory presence. They challenge you to embrace a heightened image of fictive life that differs markedly from strict realism. Your judging standards accommodate those amplified dimensions within the performance text.

Highly abstracted and stylized performances often employ ruptures in time, space, and causality to make their expressive points and thus stretch your evaluative parameters beyond realism. Even in these instances, however, it is useful to remember that all performances fall somewhere on a continuum between realism (or naturalism) at one end and elaborate stylization at the other. You pursue many of the same determinations insofar as internal consistency and relevance are concerned, but you always rate their importance in accord with the larger performance style, its efficacy and its reach. Thus, a so-called anachronism in a musical or a slap-stick farce can be seen as appropriate simply because it is more immediately tied to the "performance moment" and its effect on your perceptions than to an external referent. Your appraisal of theatrical effectiveness, the impact of the performance on your inner life, is ultimately the measuring stick of the performance's quality. When voicing your judgments you do well to list specific examples juxtaposed against the expectations the performance led you to assume. Similarly, the recommendations you make should be consistent within the parameters set out in the performance.

ADVICE COUCHED AS SUGGESTIONS RATHER THAN EDICTS

Staging recommendations you proffer to the performance team are most effective if they are couched in modest rather than insistent terms. When you preface your suggestions with "Had you considered . . .?" or "You might want to think about . . ." you do not unseat the team's author-ity to make the final decisions, and that increases the likelihood of your alternatives being seriously considered. Those recommendations that are seriously considered, whether ultimately accepted or rejected, expand the perspectives of the developing theatre artists. Your recommendations are practical (and hypothetical) re-stagings. You may sense that a major character could profit from more spectator attention being paid her in a particular scene. One suggestion might deal with a change in costume, or a different blocking pattern, or some other performance text adjustment that would accomplish that end.

Your recommendation for another scene might focus on the amount of sympathy a character might elicit from an audience just prior to being unmasked as a villain. Such an adjustment could maximize the impact of the story's sudden reversal. In almost all cases your suggestions stem from issues of relative performance text emphasis. They are usually minor al-terations that fit within the paradigm established by the performance itself.

The evaluative judgments and the suggestions you articulate to the performance team inevitably grow out of your training and experience. They are ready indexes of who you are as a theatre artist. This guidebook does not offer much in the way of aesthetic directives, although some do creep in. The assumption that informs what is being said here is that you are a qualified and thoughtful theatre artist who is undertaking to pass insights on to others. The book primarily offers guidance to making your response to *performance* open and free and useful to the developing artists who listen to you. It suggests some preferred ways to think and talk about theatre performance but does little to change your personal beliefs in the standards of excellence you have come to embrace. Nonetheless, there are some performance-specific characteristics that you will want to bear in mind when you respond to particular performances. Here, for illustrative purposes, is a sampling of some suggestible characteristics, presented in random order, that I persistently believe are worth considering.

IMMEDIACY

Typically, one of those crucial characteristics is the performance's power to simulate immediacy and spontaneity. Theatrical performance is inevitably a time-based phenomenon. Ideally, each moment in that time continuum manifests its own sense of "now." That "now" can be injudiciously muted if any participant, whether it be actor, director, technician or spectator, sacrifices the essence of the present moment to the power of the impending next (or any other) moment. Actors who anticipate an as-yet-nonexistent stimulus by flinching before they are slapped or glancing at the place where a character will soon make a "surprise" entrance blunt the sense of the ever present "now" that is almost always crucial to a performance's fragile magic. Similarly characters who rattle off their lines with no hesitancy or apparent need to think of what to say next—regardless of the stress they face—run the risk of seeming pre-programmed and not "in the moment." Characters who appear to speak by rote or fail to listen to their fellow characters subvert the performance's spontaneous texture. Directors who anticipate a play's climactic moment by telegraphing it prematurely rob the performance of its exciting conclusion. A lighting technician who brings up the light level before it is emotionally justified by the performance contributes to a syncopated and less effective sense of "now." Precise execution of timing that makes each nanosecond of behavior seem spontaneous is a prime characteristic of praiseworthy acting, just as it is for directing and technical execution. Your evaluation response is likely to spend some energy on the seeming spontaneity of the performance, the ways it was effected, and the extent to which it captured and directed your attention.

SELF DETERMINATION

Closely related to your assessment of spontaneity is your appraisal of the locus of generative energy. In most instances, performances that work seem to the spectator to derive their motive energy from within. For example, the characters seem to be the "authors" of impulses, ideas, discoveries and decisions rather than having them apparently proceed from some external agent such as the playwright or director. As a practicing theatre artist you know this perception of self determination is illusory, the whole of a show is actually conceived and charted by other than the characters. But in the fictive world all seems determined by the characters or—in special ways— the natural forces that you perceive directly as being active determinants of the "now." If this is not the case, chances are you get the feeling that you are being manipulated. This feeling wars with the fragile magic at work in the performance. At stake is nothing less than your belief in the characters' and the story's inherent credibility. Your performance evaluation justifiably takes all of this into account, with the greatest approbation typically reserved for performances which manifest their own sense of vital life.

CLARITY

Of course clarity is valued in a performance. A clear understanding of what forces are at work in the fictive world and how they interact is always highly regarded by auditors. But often the most important moment of clarity generated by a performance is eventual rather than immediate. That is, since a performance traces the arc of an experience that concludes in understanding it necessarily follows that for the spectator what can be called the embedded meaning of a performance is less clear early than late. Audience interest and the willingness to stay engaged is enhanced if the performance's plotting is viewed as similar to a concatenated series of implied questions that gradually bring the desired emotional state or satisfying answer into undeniably clear focus. Paradoxically, a performance that "works" often sows uncertainty and confusion in its early life in order to throw the eventual clarity into sharp relief. This fact emphasizes the need for the respondent to withhold terminal judgment until all the data are in.

HARMONY

Harmonious consistency in a performance text is also highly pursued by the members of the performance team and is highly regarded by the members of the audience. Whether that consistency is found in the observable behavior of a single character or in the harmony with which the costumes, settings and props support a consistent image of a fictive era, it is a potent performance quality. Your judgment about the consistency of a performance is testimony to its controlled nature.

BOLDNESS

Theatrical performance in general seems to thrive on flamboyance and a discernible audacity. Plot moments, lines of dialogue, strongly motivated characters, and conflict driven situations are among the elements that are likely to be larger than life. They throw key aspects of the performance into sharp relief. Of course, too much exaggeration and an unwarranted "over the top" quality can be distractions that undercut the effect of the performance. As a respondent you take the subjective measure of these elements and appraise their impact both within the performance and on your overall perceptions.

VIRTUOSITY

Any displays of performance virtuosity such as, for example, outstanding dancing or singing within a musical or a hair-raising sword fight in a period piece are deserving of your evaluations. The same can be said of particularly evocative costumes or surprising special effects, either aural or visual. In short, any part of the performance text which exceeds audience expectations in a calculated display of excellence lends a quality to the performance which automatically becomes noteworthy and can figure prominently in your appraisal.

Of course there are other root characteristics of performance not mentioned here that will occur to you. Not all of the characteristics noted here, nor the additional ones that you can list, will seem relevant to each of your appraisals. But keeping them in mind will assist you to phrase your commentary in ways that can help the developing theatre artists place their own efforts in larger and more telling contexts.

Theatre artists like you who serve—or aspire to serve—as effective theatre respondents are a special breed. In effect all of you set out to capture lightning in a bottle. Because you already function as artists you know at first hand what the fragile magic of theatre performance is like. You also know how frustrating it is to communicate meaningfully about it. But because you want to nurture that sense of magic in others and help pass it along you are willing to confront the formidable task of thinking and talking about theatre performance in fruitful ways, ways that preserve its essential quality. You are selflessly willing to put your aesthetic sensibility in the service of developing artists so that they may see how their own magic may be sparking in them and in their work.

WHAT'S IN IT FOR YOU

But doing all this is not entirely a selfless task. Every time you articulate a clear insight about a theatre performance that "works" you grow in your own right as well as help others to grow. The precepts laid out in this guidebook provide a modest but reasonable method for making theatre performance response an effective undertaking. I hope they serve you well. But more than that, I hope they stimulate you to find additional ways to capture that special lightning in a bottle so that developing theatre artists can be the true beneficiaries of your talents and artistry.

7

FREQUENTLY ASKED QUESTIONS

During workshops devoted to teaching the approach to performance response espoused here there are often questions. Below is a sampling of some of those most frequently asked. I hope you find them instructive.

1. Should I read the script before seeing the performance?

It is not so much a question of whether or not to read the script in advance as it is what impact doing so will have on your openness as a spectator. It is important to stay open to the performance team's vision and not to enter the viewing already committed to a particular perspective. If you can read the script in advance and remain open-minded there is no reason to avoid reading (or having other prior contact with) the script. But you must make every effort to give yourself over to the performance you witness rather than to your prior thoughts about the script.

2. Should I take notes during the performance? If so, how?

Notes taken during the performance prove very useful. First of all they minimize the strain you will feel trying to remember everything after the performance is over and you are delivering your commentary. They also preserve the arc of feelings and thought you experienced as the performance was unwinding. The changes in your perceptions and feelings that transpire during the performance reveal an important dimension of its operation. A mere summary of the final moment of the show undercuts that time-oriented aspect of theatrical performance.

However, there are cautions about note-taking you should heed. You should not let the note-taking interfere with your moment-by-moment tracking of the show. The notes should be terse and you should not labor to produce sentence-like statements. Key words are what you should transcribe, just enough to jog your memory later at which time you can elaborate on them.

There are also some practical issues to deal with in taking notes. Most probably you will be writing in the dark or with minimal light. You do not want to cause a distraction for other audience members and so the use of a penlight, especially turning it on and off, is discouraged. There are pens which themselves light up with a minimal glow and these can be used. One problem to overcome is the tendency to write one note on top of another rendering them both unreadable. I find that holding the writing surface with my left thumb indicating where I am writing (I am right-handed) works well. I then slide my thumb down a bit after the note is written and thus mark the starting place for the next note. A little practice makes this an automatic procedure and works pretty well.

3. Why is it so important to make the description non-valuative?

There are several reasons why the description you provide should be non-valuative. First of all it provides an "objective" statement of what you believe you witnessed. Since your witnessing may not exactly tally with what the team intended this makes it clear to them where you are coming from, what you are evaluating and it gives them data they can use in their self-evaluation. Your description also lays bare your sense of how the various theatre languages were employed.

When you offer a non-valuative description it defers the urge performance team members may have to know "how they did" or if "you liked it." Evaluation that comes too soon can easily interfere with their fuller understanding of the performance's functioning. By front loading your commentary with description you keep them listening.

Your non-valuative description also gives you a last minute chance to review your perception of the performance before you offer evaluations. With preparation time often very limited this can be welcomed.

4. How long should the response commentary be?

There is no firm answer to that question. Different performances make differing demands and different performance team auditors have differing expectations. As long as you have fresh and useful things to point out and they have interest and patience the response commentary can profitably proceed. In practical terms an hour is likely to be the outside limit, but shorter commentaries are the general rule. You should be sensitive to the feedback you get from the performance team and be able to adjust the length of your session accordingly.

5. Why do you use the term "performance team?"

I phrase it this way because I want to include all the many people who have some kind of active influence on the performance you witness. To be sure, some—like the playwright, the designers, the director, and the actors—are more obviously pro-active than others. But the efforts of the technicians, front of house personnel, and publicists also count and I want to draw attention to, and take into account, the nature of their possible influence.

6. What if the performance team wants to tape (audio or video) the commentary?

I think taping the response is a useful thing to do. It allows the performance team to revisit the commentary after their emotions have subsided.

7. What do you mean when you talk about a play's "arc of action?"

That is probably the toughest question to answer satisfactorily. But I'll try—one more time. Let me start by saying what I am *not* referring to when I use the word "action" in this way. I am not referring to lots of physical movement so that sitting and talking has no action and running around and yelling has lots of action. I am instead referring to what I can only call "the changing is-ness" of the play, the patterned and always shifting status quo. Usually it is linked to the progress an important character makes in achieving the goal she or he has set out to pursue. But sometimes a performance's action (or "inner life," if you prefer) is independent of character motivation. For example, it can be seen as "the shifting circumstances" in which characters find themselves enmeshed.

When I refer to the "arc" I am talking about the pattern the inner life (or "action") etches in time. We are habituated to a kind of arch-shaped pattern which we typically call an "arc," but the pattern can really have different shapes.

8. Do I behave any differently for a new script?

Original scripts sometimes present a special circumstance since respondents are often urged to read the new play first so as to be able to focus on playwriting issues somewhat apart from the performance dynamics. Even in these cases, however, it is important to distinguish between the impact of the play as performed and the play as read. Remember, your focus as a performance respondent is "performance-centric." The effectiveness of a script in performance is a valuable measure of its theatre worthiness.

9. **Does it make a difference if there is more than one respondent at a performance?**

It can make a difference if you differ from the other respondent(s). Your obligation is to provide your honest response to the performance. Varied opinions make it evident that different perspectives can operate simultaneously. Arguing with another respondent or defending your response beyond making it clear should be avoided so as not to polarize the situation.

10. **Why not conduct the response session by dealing with the team's questions?**

Often a response session can profitably incorporate a question and answer session. But to do so exclusively runs the risk of omitting issues that you, as a knowledgeable theatre artist, feel are important to the developing artists' growth.

11. **How should I respond if someone insists on asking if I liked the show?**

Try to avoid making any wholesale and summary statements that keep the details of the performance from being carefully considered. Most of the time carefully qualified observations of limited details can be offered that can defuse insistent demands for simplistic judgments.

12. **Why not conduct the response by asking questions of the performance team?**

Questioning the performance team tends to put them on the defensive and changes the topic from "the effectiveness of the performance as witnessed by a willing spectator" to "the performance team's conscious intentions and perceptions." In general think of yourself as taking a test when you witness a performance rather than giving a test by making the performance team justify themselves.

However, a skilled respondent can explore topics through questions late in the response that are entirely in keeping with good theatre response. Those questions come after the respondent has offered a detailed reaction to the performance.

13. I find it hard to be non-valuative in my comments. Is there an easy way to do this?

There is probably no easy way for you to phrase non-valuative comments if you find it difficult. It takes careful self-monitoring or perhaps helpful feedback from a willing assistant. It requires overcoming a long-standing habit whereby evaluations are the first things that come to mind. For what it is worth, I find it seems easier for people to identify others making valuative comments than to avoid making them themselves or even recognizing that their comments are valuative. With practice it will get easier for you to develop non-valuative reactions and employ a non-valuative vocabulary. Every step in that direction is helpful to you.

14. What do I do if someone gets angry?

Sometimes that happens. There is no way to guarantee that it won't happen. The best thing to do is make it clear that your responses are honest and that you acknowledge others may see things differently. Avoid being defensive and insisting on your being right. If someone judges you to be inept, sometimes you may have to let their judgment stand, but you needn't agree with it. You simply do your best to avoid its being right.

15. How can I do a response in a very short time—like three minutes?

Sometimes the exigencies of a festival force a very brief response time. You can offer the same basic commentary sequence (description of fictive world, theatre languages, and your fictive world-based thoughts and feelings followed by your evaluations) in highly limited fashion. You clearly have to focus on the most important issues. It may not feel ideal or comprehensive, but the key elements of your response can still be in place to promote the developing artists' growth.

16. What if I really hated/loved the performance?

Bear in mind that your theatre knowledge and your theatre based skills are more valuable aids to the developing artist than is your personal preference regarding the show. If you follow the outline sketched out in this guidebook the performance team will profit from your insights. But though your comments should be temperate you should not lie to your auditors. If there is good reason for your strong reactions they deserve to know them.

17. Should I sit in a particular place in the auditorium?

Very often your seat will be selected for you by your hosts. If not, it is often useful to sit in a place that is typical of regular audience positioning. It should not pose special acoustic or visual challenges or benefits. I find it useful to occupy an aisle seat owing to my note-taking needs, but that is not always essential.

18. What happens if I have to go to the restroom during the performance?

You go, as unobtrusively as possible. This situation emphasizes the need to think ahead prior to the show in order to avoid, whenever possible, interruptions of this sort.

19. What happens if I start to cough during the performance?

Ideally you will want to carry cough drops to enable you to do your job with a minimum of intrusion affecting yourself or others. This may not always be possible, but common sense is what is called for here.

20. I find your "system" too complicated and hard to execute. What should I do?

Don't try to force yourself to use the "system." Finally the approach espoused here is not simply a bundle of techniques. It articulates one way of undertaking the important task of being a theatre respondent. This approach has worked for many and it represents a perspective that I have found useful and you may as well. In the final analysis, you should simply use as much of it as makes sense to you and proves useful in your quest to help developing theatre artists.

21. You said the response system has relevance for non-respondents. What do you mean?

This may be a topic better suited for a book on its own, but here goes:

Let's start with the spectator or general audience member. Most people who attend the theatre do so without any attempt to prepare their response habits or discipline the way they allow themselves to think about (or talk to themselves) about the performance. Their responses, whether pleasurable or not, are kind of catch as catch can. If they feel a pressure to "get right to it" (by which they usually mean "meaning.") they may make snap judgments which blunt their responsiveness to later developments in the performance. They may also fall back on what they know about textual meaning and thus cut themselves off from a lot of non-verbal theatrical expressiveness.

However, if they train themselves to view non-valuatively and defer their judgmental assessments of "how good it was" they give the performance a better chance of accessing their imaginations and thought processes. In other words, taking steps to keep yourself open as a spectator is precisely what the respondent does in order to be maximally effective. For both it means setting aside those inhibiting thoughts and expectations that diminish the performance's power of accessing a spectator's imagination. Often a variant of this approach is referred to as "the willing suspension of disbelief," but it really goes beyond what is understood by that time-worn phrase.

Teachers who work directly with developing artists can profit from the admonition to empower their charges in a fashion similar to that employed by the respondent. By encouraging students to self evaluate and accept responsibility for artistic behaviors the teacher fosters a sense of aesthetic independence in them that advances their ability to accept responsibility for their own growth.

Of course the improvement of empathic skills and balanced open thinking goes well beyond theatre applications. This approach can have a salutary impact on general non- theatre-based behaviors as well.

APPENDIX

The following guide notes provide a brief overview of the principles informing the book. They can be used for a quick review before actually undertaking a performance response.

I. THEATRE ART

A. Illusion-making

Theatre creates an image of an alternate reality via a performance text. Everything that is perceptible in the production contributes to the performance text. The fictive world that is set forth in the performance text may closely resemble the world we live in or it may be wildly different. It may be precise and detailed, or it may be stylized and abstracted. But it is always a constructed reality, however alluring or forbidding.

B. Time/Space Dependent

Theatre events take place in real time and space. Things in the fictive world (people, relationships, awarenesses, convictions, etc.) change as the performance text unfolds through time. A production can also manipulate space, ignoring it or twisting it into a language of its own.

C. Collaborative

A performance text is created by many specialists (writer, designers, director, actors, etc.) working closely together. Sometimes it is difficult—if not impossible—to isolate the precise affective contribution each specialist makes to the complex illusion the audience perceives.

II. THEATRE PARA-AESTHETICS

A. Environmental Ambiance

Production circumstances influence audience's perceptions. Among the environmental factors are the size and attractiveness of the auditorium, its temperature and smells, the outside noise level, even the location of the theatre within the town or city.

B. Theatre Workers' Influence

Box office personnel, house managers, and ushers influence audience receptivity. Normally audiences like to feel welcome, safe, and comfortable.

C. Audience Tenor

The moods and behaviors of audience members have influence. Attitudes can be infectious or off-putting. For example, members of a theatre party, all of whom know each other and interact overtly, can tellingly affect the surrounding audience. Similarly, a pervasive feeling of celebration can boost an audience's responsiveness.

III. THEATRE SPECTATORSHIP

A. Reactive (Inner and Outer)

An audience member is largely reactive, attending to what is seen and heard. But any audience member, behaving both as an individual and as part of a group, is affected by more than external stimuli. Predispositions and prior attitudes play an enormous part in every reaction. They shape both what is perceived and how it is valued.

B. Interpretive

"Meaning" an audience member perceives as being "in" a production is really a product of interpretation. It develops from the audience member's filtering of production stimuli through knowledge, dispositions and attitudes. Meaning and value are transactions rather than characteristics; they are 'in" the audience member as much as they are "in" the production.

IV. THEATRE FESTIVAL DYNAMICS

A. Celebratory

A festival celebrates. Tribute is paid to the art of theatre and fellow workers; common interests are celebrated.

B. Educational

Participants want to learn about theatre. They seek evaluations of past (present) work and ideas as to what to consider for the future. Greater practical educational value comes from what can be applied to future productions.

C. Social

Theatre always has a strong social dimension. People congregating invoke a sense of a production's significance and worth. Auditors structure the dynamics of their own interaction. Festivals are especially powerful socially.

D. Competitive

Festivals almost always induce a spirit of competition. If shows are being ranked or selected for future performance, competition is especially strong.

V. THEATRE RESPONDENT

A. Fellow Theatre Worker

A respondent is usually a fellow theatre worker filling the specialized role of adjudicator briefly. After the festival, the respondent will probably resume doing what the festival participants are doing, making theatre.

B. Responsible Witness

A respondent witnesses the production as openly and fully as possible. The respondent then shares those honest observations usefully—clearly and tactfully.

C. Knowledgeable

A respondent has a background in theatre that provides a valuable knowledge base on which to draw. That knowledge is marshaled on behalf of the event being witnessed.

D. Communicative

A respondent should have the ability to communicate insights and perspectives appropriate to the theatre event in a clear, concise, and tactful manner. Because tastes in theatre are both intensely personal and likely to vary widely this is not always easy to do.

E. Presumed Authority

A respondent typically is respected and has worthy insights, but it is dangerous to accept or assume too much authoritative power. The people ultimately responsible for a work of theatre art are its creators.

VI. An Approach to Adjudication/Response

A. Description

The initial section of a respondent's presentation is non-evaluative and descriptive. Without registering personal taste, the respondent describes three things that in turn empower the participants and lets them know the ways their production affected "a fellow theatre worker committed to honest and full witnessing of their work."

1. The Fictive World

Describe the fictive world: its time and place, its familiarity and uniqueness, the forces that operate in it, and the nature and behavior of the characters who populate it—what they do, how they do it, and how they fare. This differs from telling the plot, although it may refer to it. It describes the fictive world as seen on the stage via the performance text.

2. The Theatrical Means

Describe, as best you can, the theatrical stimuli that revealed the fictive world. Deal with various theatre specialists—designers (costume, lights, sound, settings), director, actors, etc—by describing how their efforts evoked a response.

3. Intellectual and Emotional Impressions

Describe, in terms of the fictive world, what you thought and felt as the production unfolded. Pay particular attention to how your impressions of happenings and significance underwent changes. This is not a statement of how well or poorly you think any theatre worker performed.

B. Evaluation

"Evaluation" and "Recommendation" are usually combined.

1. Standards

Describe expectations you feel are appropriate to the production. Consider both those the production generated in you and those you arrived with and were not induced to alter. You might, for example, include such things as consistency of character behavior; harmony of locale and behavior; congruence of historical period, manners, and dress; credibility of unfolding moods; etc. Typically these are the bases on which we regard things as right or wrong, better or worse.

2. Responses

Explain how you (1) endorse, (2) accept grudgingly, (3) cannot understand, or (4) cannot accept specific aspects of the performance text. These evaluative responses should be linked to the standards—mentioned above—you regarded as appropriate. These are the things themselves you regard as right or wrong, better or worse. But, expressed in the context of the standards you are applying, they are treated as expressive and communicative devices rather than inflexible shibboleths.

C. Recommendation

As a way of reactivating the participants' creative thought processes, recommend alternatives you think might avoid problematic performance text shortcomings. Of course, you have no way of knowing whether or not your recommendations will work, nor whether or not they were already tried by the company and found wanting. But you are not trying to come up with solutions that are foolproof. You are trying to clarify your observations in the trial and error, imaginative, "what if" way used by theatre artists everywhere. Properly (that is, clearly and tactfully) articulated, such recommendations or suggestions can remind the participants of the assumptions and rationales that informed their production choices. You can reactivate their earlier creative state whereupon they can reimagine and re-envision their show, and, perhaps more importantly, invoke an enhanced creative state for the next project.

VII. Some Final Observations About Adjudication/Response

The key to effective response is more attributable to attitude than to a cluster of specific techniques. A respondent performs a valuable service, that of providing outside eyes and informed taste, for fellow theatre workers. By describing as fully as possible what illusion was seen, what means were used to create that illusion, and what the inner workings of that illusion did to a responsive and thoughtful witness, the respondent gives participants invaluable information. The amplification of that gift through the respondent's evaluative response, suggestions, and statement of applicable standards continues the service. Thoughtful participants will draw upon that fund of information when creating their next work—and frankly, that is where it counts.

But the respondent is not a know-it-all seer and should avoid being seduced into accepting that role, whoever offers it. Moreover, any respondent who can devise other techniques and approaches to reach out and help, in a non-threatening and productive way, fellow theatre workers to achieve theatre excellence should do so. Training in or use of specific response techniques does not automatically make one wise about theatre. Some respondents are effective simply because their personalities make clear that the insights they are offering are freely and joyously given. Their presentations may not follow the form outlined above. So what? What we all want is good theatre and a better way of sharing with each other the best of our thoughts and feelings about something we mutually cherish.